SURVIVING BABIES & TODDLERS

Congrats on the
new baby!
Keep Surviving!
Joel
3/19/21

SURVIVING BABIES & TODDLERS

By Joel Houston

ENDEAVOR
LITERARY PRESS

Surviving Babies and Toddlers
Copyright © 2020 by Joel Houston

Published by Endeavor Literary Press
P.O. Box 49272
Colorado Springs, Colorado 80949
www.endeavorliterary.com

ISBN Print Version: 978-1-7358671-0-6
ISBN Ebook: 978-1-7358671-1-3

Cover Design: James Clarke (jclarke.net)

Contents

About the Author

Joel Houston is a native of Washington State. He has a bachelor's degree in economics and an MBA from Pacific Lutheran University. At the apex of his career he sold his warehousing business and became a full-time parent.

Recently, Joel and Katie relocated to the Jersey Shore, which required a three-thousand-mile drive with two kids, a dog, a turtle, and a boat. When he is not managing the kids' video conference classes, homework, and activities, Joel writes about trying to survive life.

So far, so good.

Acknowledgements

First, I would like to acknowledge my wife and partner in all things, Katie. She changed about thirty thousand diapers so that I could write a book about that.

Second, I would like to acknowledge my mom and dad. If it were not for them, I would not be here. For the sake of my sanity, it is best not to dwell on the details of how that happened.

Third, I would like to acknowledge my mother-in-law. She gets credit for babysitting during most of the "date nights" Katie and I have had since we became parents—much to her regret.

Foreword

By Katie Houston

My life changed the morning I woke up and took a pregnancy test. I was shocked that it was positive. I felt and looked the same, and there was not much fanfare. But it was a momentous morning.

The first phases of pregnancy—discovering the gender, the name game, the nursery décor—were fun. I was slightly preoccupied by the fact that I would soon be carrying a watermelon-size baby. That reality seemed totally unfair. In fact, I contemplated the advantages of hens, which only need to lay small eggs.

During pregnancy, I imagined what it would be like to be a mom. I gradually learned that my vision would have nothing to do with Reality. I had assumed that my children would be like me.

I had been a calm, bookish child who was quiet, respectful, and loved to draw. I had not envisioned that my first child would be extremely curious, physically active, loud, and outgoing. I had also assumed that my second child would be like the first. I now know that children are more like snowflakes; no two are the same and you can't predict what you are going to get.

I can proudly say that I have survived babies and toddlers, which is remarkable when I consider what I went through. My Facebook history from a few years ago allowed me to relive some of the greatest hits. A few actual posts are shown below.

> *November 7:* Ugh, the time change strikes again. Baby Aedan got up at 5 a.m. Then, for good measure, he socked me in the nose at about 6 a.m.

> *January 24:* Observations after having spent 36+ hours without power: changing diapers while clenching a flashlight between your teeth is interesting to say the least.

> *October 3:* Can I start his day over? This morning Cujo (our dog) left me tootsie roll presents from one end of the family room to

the other. As Joel put it, it was if the dog had exploded all over the room. How can one little dog poop so much? And now Aedan just threw a dog toy into one of my nice china pepper shakers and it blew up into shards of China and pepper everywhere. Kid/dog tag-team: 2. Me: 0

December 8: Ten nights in a row of watching *The Boss Baby* movie, and it is still like new for Brennan.

December 18: Playing Jenga with a three-year-old and a six-year-old. What could possibly go wrong?

Joel and I are still in the middle of the journey and making more memories every day. The kids have outgrown their old tricks just in time to practice new ones. I hope you enjoy reading about our experiences. We don't care if you laugh with us or *at us,* as long as you're laughing.

And Then There Were Three

Katie and I took the CPR, newborn prep, and baby massage classes. Our baby was two-weeks late, so we set the date to induce labor. We had the crib and the changing table. The baby's room was painted. We bought clothes, diapers, food, bottles, booties, a diaper genie, a swing, travel playpen, and pee-pee teepees. We also had the bottle warmer, bottle sterilizer, diaper bag, car seat, baby wipes, baby vibrator chair, burp cloths, jumper, and baby gym. If Babies-R-Us sold it, we bought at least one and sometimes two (just in case).

We were woefully unprepared . . . for everything.

Start with a Name

Before we bought the gear, we decided on a temporary name: Dallas Austin. We needed a name because the instant people learned the baby's sex, they asked, "What's his name?" We also knew that if we didn't have a name, we would get unwelcome suggestions. Even with a temporary name, people bombarded us with feedback, opinions, recommendations, and sometimes tears. Mere acquaintances believed they had a stake in the name game.

We thought everyone would understand that the temporary name, Dallas Austin, was a joke. (If *you* don't get it, review my last name.) But we were wrong. Even the soon-to-be grandparents didn't think it was funny.

The root of our problem was that we didn't yet have a *permanent* name. The potential names we threw out were immediately met with jokes or derision. Numerous relatives complained because the child might not be named after a family member, meaning *them*. It takes balls to insist that someone else's baby be named after you. Nevertheless, when we told the relatives that we didn't like their ideas and that we didn't want suggestions, they took offense and continued to harp on us. But we didn't care. This was our decision, and ours alone. Communicating this fact to everyone was a daily battle, one we did not anticipate.

How were we going to make the decision for a real name? It turned out that Katie and I couldn't come to an agreement, even after weeks of scouring the internet for baby names. So, I devised a simple game. We each put ten names on a list, for a total of twenty. Then we each got to veto five of the other person's names, paring the list down to five from each of us.

For the next round, we each got to number the names from one to ten in order of preference, with the lowest number being most preferred. We added the two scores together for each name and took the five names with the lowest combined scores. For the third round we numbered the five remaining names from one to five, with the lowest number still being most preferred. Then we added the scores for each name. The name with the lowest score was the winner. It happened to be the name I wanted most: Aedan. Another name I wanted, Sawyer, became the baby's middle name because Katie liked it.

The outcome was never really in doubt (for me). After reading a game theory book for a college economics class, I learned that when there are multiple scoring rounds, I could manipulate the vote to get the results I wanted. Eventually, after we had chosen a name, I confessed to Katie how I had manipulated the game. Thankfully, she was happy with the results, but only *if* she could use her preferred name for our second child (if we had another boy). I agreed, so we named our second son Brennan Finn. You might recognize the Sawyer-Finn connection from literature class. Katie and I still disagree on whose idea it was to name the boys after Tom Sawyer and Huckleberry Finn, but we each take credit.

As we should have expected, our relatives weren't too pleased when they heard that we had named our first son Aedan. My relatives and Katie's wanted us to use their names. Katie is a third generation Kathleen, so if we had had a girl, the pressure would have been immense to name the baby Kathleen. Thankfully, we never had to face that battle.

There were, however, other battles, such as protecting my wife's body from strangers during her pregnancy.

Belly Rubbing and Lady Parts

If you like people to touch your belly, get pregnant. Strangers touch your stomach without asking for permission. During Katie's pregnancy, a plethora of coworkers, TSA agents, family members, and random strangers copped a feel.

So, Katie started wearing a shirt with big block letters that said, "DON'T TOUCH THE BELLY." People did it anyway, with a feverish gleam in their eyes. They couldn't control themselves. Her pregnant belly was like a magnet with powers to shut down cognitive functions and attract hands.

Katie soon learned to recognize the look of belly rubbers as they approached. In those cases, she'd say, "Don't touch me." But it didn't always stop them. Every person who touched her belly without asking for permission, or in direct defiance of Katie's directives, was female. Only one guy touched her belly, but he asked for and received permission first.

Katie had to endure other complications. Every bathroom trip prompted comments. Katie's boss would say, "Running the gauntlet, I see," as she scurried down the hall. Her grandfather, Popo, tirelessly asked, "Smuggling watermelons again?"

It got worse as Katie got closer to the due date. No topic was taboo. Coworkers started asking *me* how dilated she was. "I don't know," was my confused reply. When Katie realized that I was getting questions about her lady parts, she gave me instructions for how to reply. "Please don't talk to people about my heart-shaped box and do not use the V word," she said. (What term was I supposed to use?)

I'm not the type of guy who talks to anyone about my wife's naughty bits. I don't even want to discuss the status of her "muff" with *her.* I'd rank that conversation right down there with topics about her weight. Those issues are better left buried in the backyard or tossed into Puget Sound with cement shoes.

Unfortunately, such topics during pregnancy are unavoidable. During every doctor's appointment, the staff weighed her and made her pee in a cup to make sure she didn't have gestational diabetes. They looked at her "pink Cadillac" and conversed about its condition. They stuck needles in her to draw blood and they stuck needles in her to inject vitamins and iron. She felt like a human pincushion. I took her to most of the appointments, so I had a front-row seat. It wasn't what I wanted to do, but she wanted my moral support. If she wanted me there to discuss dilation, then I was going to be there to discuss dilation.

Then there was the list of banned foods. It pained her to hear that many soft cheeses were *verboten*. No deli meat because of listeria. No Caesar salad because of raw eggs in the dressing. No fish because of the mercury. No cold pizza from the fridge. *All* food had to be microwaved to kill bacteria.

Katie also decided that chicken tasted weird, so that was out. When we finally figured out what she could eat and wanted to eat, we concluded that the child would be a pasta baby. Katie ate pasta mixed with cheddar cheese and parmesan cheese almost every night for months. I wasn't going to argue, but sometimes I'd make the pasta for her and then make myself something different. I'm a fan of pasta, but this was ridiculous.

Prep Me

As pasta fueled the baby's growth, the time came for us to take a childbirth class. The newborn prep class was about a month before the due date.

We learned that we could not use some of the baby gear we had purchased, including the baby crib blankets, baby crib bumper, and baby powder. Had we only known . . .

The required classes were offered by the hospital where our baby would be born. I'm glad we took them. Katie had already changed a diaper or two, but I had never held or fed a baby, much less changed a diaper. As a young adult, I had kept my distance from babies. The noise, the smell, the fragility—no thanks. The words I least wanted to hear were, "I'm pregnant and you're the father." Even when I was growing up, when people tried to hand me their babies, I defensively held up my hands and said, "I don't want to drop it."

So, the prep class helped us a lot. However, some other soon-to-be moms made Katie envious. One was past her due date but you couldn't even tell she was pregnant. She was tall and thin and probably moonlighted as a model for fashion magazines. She was bothersome for Katie, who with a month to go had gained more weight than she had wanted.

Katie was also jealous of another pregnant gal who was having twins and who already had a C-section scheduled to get them out. This woman would get two children (our goal) with just one pregnancy, and she would not need to destroy her nether regions to do it. She also would not face a pregnancy horror story, such as a three-day labor.

During Katie's pregnancy, everyone shared a horror story with us. Three-day labors. Poop explosions. Blood fountains. Goat sacrifices. Baby looked like the best man instead of the husband. Doctor had a heart attack in the middle of the delivery. The baby died. The mom died. The mom *and* the baby died. The anesthesiologist was sick, so mom had to endure a natural delivery without pain blockers. No one had any *good* stories. Or perhaps no one shared those because they were boring.

The Delivery

We were as prepared for labor and delivery as any first-time parents could be, which isn't saying much. Katie and I were at the hospital at 6 a.m. We expected inducement and labor to be an all-day process (or longer). So, after she settled into the room, she sent me home to let the dogs out and kill some time. Katie was awesome. She had her HGTV shows to watch anyhow.

I was back at the hospital at about 5 p.m. when

Katie began to dilate. Soon it was time to begin pushing. The nurse instructed me to grab one of Katie's legs while the nurse grabbed the other. I did as the nurse asked, but I was a little surprised that I would be participating so directly. I had pictured myself standing off to the side while Katie yelled at me. "You will never be allowed to touch me again!" That's what happens in the movies, right?

Whenever I share how difficult it was to hold Katie's leg, I generally get a smart-ass comment, such as, "Oh yeah, *you* had the hard job," followed by, "Asshole." But I never compared my "suffering" to my wife's labor. I know I had the easy part. I would not have traded places with my wife for $100,000. At $1 million, I'd still say no. For $10 million, I'd consider it. There are a lot of things I'd do for $10 million.

And that reminds me of a joke I've seen going around Facebook. Some guy says, "You know, getting kicked in the balls must hurt more than labor because no guy ever says, 'Kick me in the nuts again.' But women willingly have more than one child."

My point is this: An experienced medical professional told me to hold a leg. So that is what I did.

The best way I can explain the next two hours is to use the analogy of a horror movie. There was blood and other bodily fluids and screaming. People were running willy-nilly, and people were huddling in closets crying. I was crying. Katie told me to knock off the crying and do what the nurse told me to do. Katie was on drugs and highly motivated to end the horror movie as quickly as possible. Smuggling a watermelon in her stomach had gotten old months ago.

Our baby was born just before 11 p.m. that same night. He was a beautiful and healthy boy of eight pounds nine ounces. Nurses and healthcare workers paraded by for a couple of hours, all commenting about how cute our baby was. I'm sure they say that about every newborn, but it was nice to hear.

Sometime after midnight, they escorted us out of the birthing room and into the overnight suite. The nurses helped us feed the baby, showed us how to change his diaper, talked about breastfeeding, and demonstrated how to swaddle him. At first, they were angels helping us with our newborn, but after a while they became devils who prevented us from getting rest.

Despite our exhaustion, the nurses and doctors

were fantastic. Even a maternity ward security guard went out of his way to grab a sandwich for Katie from the deli. He knew she wouldn't otherwise be able to get food after delivering a baby. Katie's favorite person was the anesthesiologist who made sure she had a painless childbirth.

Visitors, as expected, arrived the next morning, including my parents (Grandma and Grandad) and Katie's mom (Grandmom). The ink was dry on the birth certificate, so they saw that their first grandchild's name was officially Aedan Sawyer.

This was our first child, so the hospital expected us to stay a second night. I went home and Grandmom stayed with Katie. There was no point in having two sleepless parents. One of us had to be fresh when the baby came home.

The hospital discharged us the next morning with a baby, some formula, a couple of diapers, and a ton of paperwork. After fumbling around with the car seat, I got the baby strapped in for a short drive. Soon we were in our quiet home, a departure from the hustle and bustle of the hospital. No one except baby, Katie, and me. The world had changed. Our baby was home.

Katie immediately went to bed. A natural birth is rough on a woman. Due to significant pain and bodily damage, recovery can take weeks. I was fortunate to be able to take a week off to support her. I wanted to be an active father, raising our children at all stages, and that meant being there for her and Aedan.

With Katie in bed, I was alone with the sleeping baby (and our two dogs). I picked up a video game controller. Before I could turn on the system, I heard Aedan's loud "wah!" It had begun. I'll tell you all about the "it," but first let me introduce baby number two.

And Then There Were Four

My poor wife had just finished losing all the weight from the first pregnancy. Her body would never be the same. While pregnant with Aedan, her feet had enlarged a whole shoe size and she had to have her wedding ring refitted. To feel normal, she had considered investing in "the mommy special": nip and tuck, liposuction, and boob job.

Now she was pregnant *again*. This meant another year without alcohol, a return to the prenatal vitamin routine, and another round of regular visits to the obstetrician. And *this* time Katie would do it all while lugging around a highly mobile toddler who still needed diaper changes, feedings, and entertainment. She would once again smuggle a watermelon in her belly. She would have to endure another horror movie with blood, crying, and screaming. She would have to push the watermelon out of her naughty bits and then face six weeks of recovery before the parts could function correctly again.

We fully understood that we were assuming another twenty-five-year commitment to take care of child number two. We were not blind to the cost of doctors, diapers, food, and clothing, which all adds up. We knew that he or she might want to go to college, and that the cost would probably bankrupt us, even after the first kid's college costs had *already* bankrupted us.

None of this came as a surprise. We now had *experience*. We knew what to expect. We had our OSHA-approved Safety-First procedures down pat. We would do everything better this time. Or so we thought.

Reality Check

When Brennan was born, we understood that newborns don't follow a schedule; but we didn't comprehend the challenge of managing a toddler at the same time.

Toddlers often sleep for eleven hours a night. So, without a newborn around, the parents can do some adulting after the kid goes to bed. We often enjoyed seven or eight hours of sleep. When the second baby arrived, that luxury vanished. Now, instead of changing just one kid's diaper, we often had to change two at the same time. Frequently, when the baby was on the changing table, our toddler would run out of sight. We could only pray that Aedan wasn't about to burn the house down. Had we remembered to take the knob off the stove after making breakfast? Sweating bullets, we would repeatedly call for the toddler before disaster could ensue. No response. Call again. Silence. We would try not to panic. Were all the doors leading out of the house still locked? Any smell of smoke? The dogs seemed fine . . .

After what seemed like an eternity, we would sometimes find the toddler hiding in our bed under the covers. Normally, the little shit wouldn't shut up, but when we happened to be freaking out about his disappearance, he became quiet as a dormouse. Apparently, he thought it was time for hide and seek. He thought it was funny to see us worked into a lather.

Upon locating the toddler, we would get the baby out of his crib. The baby had been crying the whole time because, even though we had changed his diaper, we had not yet fed him, and he was a growing boy who needed his formula *right now!* So, we'd grab the baby, take him to the kitchen, and realize that we'd lost the toddler again. We could often hear him running through the house (thump, thump, thump, thump, thump) but we couldn't see him. Paranoia would set in again, leading us to *imagine* the smell of smoke.

So, it didn't take long for Reality to set in. Our illusions quickly dissipated.

What were those illusions? Prior to Brennan's landing, we had grown weary of being Aedan's sole source of entertainment, so we searched for solutions. "I think Aedan needs a playmate," we mused. "A little brother or sister would help keep him busy. They will be best buddies. It'll be more efficient for us."

What I'm trying to say here, about Reality, about what we learned upon the birth of our second child, is that two kids would nearly break us. That is what I'm saying about Reality.

Other Considerations

Prior to the second pregnancy, our ages concerned us. We were already in our mid-thirties and few good pregnancy years remained. We definitely wanted a second child. The best time to do that was sooner, not later. And then we even considered having a third child. With the clock ticking louder, we knew we would need to get number two out of the oven so that we'd have time for number three. Three kids? That's the power of self-delusion, folks.

We expected another boy. I told Katie before we got married that my goal was three children. The first two would be boys and the third would be a girl. Katie didn't believe my bullshit for one minute. However, her obstetrician, calling it "Vegas odds," told her about the chances of having one sex or another, and it was not fifty-fifty.

In any case, I correctly predicted the second child's sex. We were going to have another boy. That was fortunate because we already had a boy's name picked out. As mentioned in chapter 1, we'd be calling the new boy Brennan Finn.

The second pregnancy and prep were different. First of all, we didn't need classes; we'd been there and done that, and now I'm literally writing the book on these topics. Another difference: Medical professionals declared that Katie was of "advanced maternal age." This condition would require more visits to specialty doctors, more tests, and more needles than the first pregnancy. She also had to constantly hear me quip about her "advanced age." She quickly got tired of those jokes, and I can't blame her. I wondered how she might get revenge. Put laxative in my food?

Modern medicine has given us, for better or worse, access to an overwhelming amount of information. In theory, more information is better. In practice, it can be hard to weed out the important information from the noise, and parents can waste time worrying about the wrong things.

Case in point: Brennan's ultrasounds showed that he was going to be a small baby with short legs. The doctor said he couldn't elaborate because he didn't know any more than that. When a doctor says "I don't know any more," I can't sleep at night.

Katie, however, saw a silver lining. She was relieved to hear that Brennan wasn't going to be a big baby, because Aedan was eight pounds nine ounces with a head circumference in the ninety-fifth percentile, and Katie is a tiny gal. It didn't seem fair to make her push out another large baby.

At thirty-eight weeks, Katie had another ultrasound. Our concerns about, and her hopes for, a small baby disappeared. Brennan was almost nine pounds. As it turns out Brennan's earlier ultrasounds merely revealed a genetic trait. He was (and is) built like me: long torso, short legs. Now we had a new worry: the size of his head. That also appeared to be my genetic fault, because my family is known for big heads. I needed custom-fit caps when I played high school baseball and people were always surprised by my head measurements. Brennan was looking to set a family head-size record. So, when the doctor asked Katie if she wanted to induce labor early, she immediately answered yes! That meant Brennan would be born a week before his due date.

There Will Be More Blood

The big day started similarly to Aedan's birth. We were at the hospital at 6 a.m. with Aedan in tow. I got Katie settled in her room and then Aedan and I went back home to hang out with the dogs. Later that day, Katie's mom came to watch Aedan and I went back to the hospital to support Katie during labor.

Brennan didn't make it easy. They monitored his vitals and, depending on Katie's posture, his heart rate would drop. She had to keep changing positions. At some point, the epidural came out and she started feeling *all* the labor pain. Thankfully, the anesthesiologist was able to reinsert the needle.

Once again, there was blood and crying (me). But soon, at 10 p.m. that day, we had our second little boy, all eight pounds and eleven ounces of him: big head (ninety-ninth percentile), long torso, short legs. Even though he arrived three weeks earlier than Aedan had, Brennan was two ounces heavier. Katie is fortunate that we didn't wait longer.

The hospital staff moved us from the birthing room to the overnight suite. This time, seeing that we had been there and done that, the nurses were less engaged with new baby care. And they scheduled us to get kicked out the next afternoon. No need to stay an extra night.

Aedan had turned three by the time Brennan was born. He got to visit his baby brother early the next morning with Grandmom. Aedan was interested but somewhat confused about the new baby. He soon decided his Kindle was more fun than a sleeping newborn.

We headed home as a complete family. I swear I heard both dogs groan when they saw Brennan. As I describe later in the book, they had good reason to be dismayed. We, however, were better mentally equipped as parents. The massive checklist of baby gear we had for Aedan was slashed dramatically for Brennan. No longer useful: baby wipe warmer, bottle warmer, pee-pee teepees, bottle sterilizer, fancy no-air bottles, the bumpo (Aedan hated it), and other things that sounded good in theory but didn't help in practice.

Having a second child was just as special as the first one, but now there was less pomp and circumstance. Being parents who had been there and done that, we didn't have the same level of excitement during some of Brennan's milestones. For example, we had documented every one of Aedan's feedings, but Brennan's usually escaped unnoticed. Who had time for ceremonies? We were trying to watch two kids simultaneously, and Aedan, then a toddler, was a disaster waiting to happen.

Now that we had a good grasp of Reality, we knew Brennan would be our last child. The three-child delusion had been beaten down by Reality. That meant that his childhood milestones would be the last we witnessed—until we became grandparents. Then we would be able to experience the fun without the grind. No need to change ten diapers per day, or get up several times a night, or worry about the toddler burning the house down. Maybe that's why, when Katie and I got married, relatives at family gatherings frequently asked, "When are you going to have kids?" Maybe one day we'll get a chance to ask our boys the same question.

How to Change a Diaper

At the end of the first chapter, I promised to explain the "it" that began when Aedan was born. From this chapter forward, I'm fulfilling that promise. "It" starts with basic digestive functions.

For every diaper I've changed, my wife has changed twenty, so she should be writing this chapter. However, this is not an expert's guide to diaper changing; rather, it is a meditation on all the ways I screwed up.

New parents are familiar with the uniqueness of the first two or three diaper changes. The first poop is like black, sticky tar and has a fancy name:

meconium. It's the most disgusting thing you've ever seen. The only thing more nauseating is every poopy diaper after the meconium. It's a universal rule: The current diaper will always be worse than the one before it.

To be honest, I didn't find the meconium to be that bad. The quantity was minimal, and it cleaned up easily with baby wipes. Unfortunately, Aedan's meconium got on my hands and I didn't like that at all. I don't remember a smell, which is fine; there were plenty of smells later.

Diaper changing, from the baby's perspective, is sheer bliss. While the parent is gagging and tearing up from the smell, the baby is the happiest of creatures. I guess you would be happy too if you shit yourself and someone else came to clean it up.

We had some diaper changing instruction prior to Aedan's birth. During the newborn class at the hospital, we practiced on a doll. Katie, because she had changed diapers on her dolls, had more experience than me. I had never played with dolls, just GI Joes and action figures, so I had never touched a diaper before.

Now, in the class, *I* was playing with dolls. It was a reasonable way to practice changing a diaper, but too theoretical. As I soon learned, a real baby does not lie still like a doll. It squirms and kicks. Worse yet, a live baby is like a loaded gun. The chamber is filled with some blanks and some live rounds. The baby shoots randomly, without warning. Whenever I took a diaper off of a real baby, I knew I was playing Russian roulette.

A Step-by-Step Guide

Diaper changing step number one is: Avoid getting the mess on yourself. That is easier said than done, but practice makes perfect. I was highly motivated to not get another human's poop on me, so I was able to figure it out. The key was to keep plenty of baby wipes within reach. Baby wipes saved my sanity—and my clothing, and my walls, and my carpet.

Step two is to get the dirty diaper in a proper receptacle without spilling the mess. Proper placement of the diaper genie, or other dirty diaper receptacle, is vital. I realized I was in trouble if getting the dirty diaper into the diaper genie would require me to step away from the baby. Stepping away from a baby to ensure proper placement of a diaper in a diaper genie would leave the baby at risk of falling off the changing table.

I also discovered that leaving a dirty diaper on a changing table was a bad idea, at least for people like me who had active newborns. Before I learned that lesson, I found myself wiping poop off the baby's foot or leg and then getting it on my hands. I almost called for backup once when that happened, but I didn't want to be "that guy." If I could change the oil in my car without soiling myself (a lie), then I could change a diaper and stay clean (also a lie).

I learned that putting the diaper on the floor was also a bad idea. Our Dachshund, Cujo, was attracted to dirty diapers like a fly to dog crap. Dogs can be exceedingly disgusting creatures, and Cujo set the gold standard for disgusting behavior. The day I realized that the dog loved dirty diapers, I used one foot to keep him at bay while I got a new diaper on Aedan and scooped him up. Then I grabbed the dirty diaper, put it in the diaper genie, and triumphantly left the room. However, I forgot to move the diaper genie closer to the changing table, leading to future ordeals.

Katie had an easier time with these types of unforeseen, surprise battles. Perhaps it was maternal instinct, or because she's smarter, but she rarely seemed intimidated. That said, she was not invincible. Even after twenty-three thousand diaper changes, she still gagged at the worst ones.

Step three of changing a diaper is probably the most important: Apply the new diaper as quickly as possible. Messing up steps one and two caused suffering, but when I made mistakes on step three, the outcome was disastrous. Turns out that cold air hitting a teeny weenie frequently triggers a geyser, also called a golden shower.

One of my big challenges was finding a way to clean myself up after getting baby mess all over me. I couldn't walk away to a bathroom because Katie and I had established a Safety-First culture in our home, which meant that I had to stay at my post, receive the golden shower without running away, and then, with pee dripping off my face and arms, complete the diaper change. Unless I had help nearby, I stayed in the trench until the end of the battle.

We bought pee-pee teepees to cover up our boys' teeny weenies. This technology kept the fountain from dousing *everything*, but it failed to prevent backsplash all over the baby, the changing table, and our hands. Also, I found that applying a pee-pee teepee took about the same time as I needed to place a new diaper over the teeny weenie.

Diapers, being absorbent, served my needs better than the teepee. Not only that, a pee-pee teepee was defenseless against a number two. A golden shower is bad, but a code brown is horrific, like a hazardous materials emergency. If OSHA were to get involved in code brown regulation, they would require reflective bodysuits, gloves, goggles, helmets, and a hazmat team.

Babies are gassy and their poop lacks consistency. This combination is not designed for safe parenting. I have cleaned sharts off a wall that was six feet away. For this reason, I dreaded having to change a diaper while visiting a friend's house. Being a considerate man, and wishing to protect the homes of my friends from sharts, I always chose to aim the weapon at myself and cross my fingers.

We have seen inconsiderate house guests, the sort of people who change a baby on the couch without protection underneath. If it was one of "those days," relations could become tense. The guest would have to explain why poop was allowed to splatter on the couch and carpet. We might have to awkwardly talk about a cleaning bill. Hard feelings could linger.

Step four is to make sure there are extra diapers on hand. Even if I had been successful with step three, I discovered that a baby could produce several vile emissions immediately after I had installed a clean diaper. This Reality reminded me of my binge drinking days. After a night of too much fun, I would need to sit on the toilet ten times in one day. Well, for a baby, every day is like that. Babies feed constantly, which means they pee and poop constantly.

It's not just the frequency. It's the volume. It shocked me to see how much a baby could poop once he got going. If I was in knee-deep, I tried to remember Safety-First protocols. If no one was around to help, I would wait until the baby had finished unloading, pick him up (getting stuff all over myself), and then get the supplies I lacked.

Blowouts were the absolute worst. My cute little babies in adorable Winnie the Pooh onesies could poop so much that the diaper could no longer contain the emission. It would creep out the leg holes and, defying gravity, *up the baby's back*. I learned how to predict if a blowout was imminent. The first sign of an impending problem was slight leakage through the onesie. Seeing this, I would grab a new outfit on my way to the changing table, which enabled me to resolve everything at once.

Step five is to yell for help. I used this method

when I screwed up all of the first four steps. If no one else was home except me, the baby, and the dog, then I would use an entire packet of baby wipes—and a smile.

I found smiling to be important. Even if I'd done things wrong, and even if I was brown and wet, I could always make sure the *baby* was clean. A clean baby is generally a happy baby. If I smiled at him, he would usually smile back. My babies never judged me, even if I had pee dripping off my nose, poop on my walls, and a Dachshund licking something off my shoe.

How to Feed a Baby

Feeding babies is part art, part science—a search for the philosopher's stone.

We started with bottle technology that was supposed to prevent air bubbles, hopefully leading to a less gassy and less burp-stricken baby. New bottle technology comes with a lot of small parts, all of which needed to be cleaned in a special sterilizing machine before each use. Putting these pieces together in the right configuration was not a simple task.

Once the dry formula had been measured and put in the bottle, we had to add the right amount of water, shake it up, and heat it for several minutes. Newborns can only drink a couple of ounces of formula at a time, so this process had to be repeated six to eight times per day, including during Dracula's hours.

We soon learned that a hungry baby will cry progressively louder the longer it takes him or her to receive food. We typically had forty-five seconds before the wail hit jet-engine decibel levels, which is to say before mirrors and windows shattered. If our bottle preparation process exceeded ten minutes, we worried that neighbors might call the authorities. There is a rumor (started by me) that the air raid alarms used in World War II were modeled on the screams of a hungry baby.

It wasn't long before we started using the simplest bottles we could find. We sterilized them in the dishwasher and gave them to the baby with cold formula. Katie could grab a bottle, throw some formula in it, add some water, put the lid on, shake the bottle, and hand it to Aedan in less than twenty-five seconds.

Gaining efficiency and experience, we prepared bottles in advance and stored them in the fridge. Our babies didn't care if the formula was cold, so why not? At their peak, each of our sons could down five, eight-ounce bottles of cold formula per day.

Using uncomplicated bottles increased delivery speed, but we created a new problem by not buying a dozen of the same brand. As we wore out bottles and bought new ones, we soon had a bunch of incompatible parts. If we mixed a cap from brand A with a bottle from brand B, we ended up with formula leaking all over the baby.

We never had any problems getting our babies to eat. We just had to be careful to not let our fingers get too close to the child's mouth lest he suck off the prints. Our boys guzzled bottles like coeds on St. Patrick's Day. We used to stand around Aedan and chant "Chug! Chug! Chug!" When he could hold his bottle, he'd finish chugging the formula and then he'd spike the bottle like a running back who had just scored a touchdown.

Burping

Burping a baby is similar to watching TV after Thanksgiving dinner with an old uncle. Uncle Charlie leans back in the recliner and, between belches, yells at the Cowboys or Lions. Then he pounds down another beer, fueling another round of burping and yelling. Good times.

Unlike disgusting Uncle Charlie, a parent must hold the baby over a shoulder and let the child burp. *Like* Uncle Charlie, the burps might be loaded. Because our babies were special, we could expect a comeback-upper every time—on our shoulders. As with changing a dirty diaper, the key is to be prepared.

Gassy babies can be unhappy babies. Katie and my mother took an infant massage class to help Aedan with this problem. When he fussed and showed discomfort, Katie massaged his abdomen, gently folded his legs, and pushed his knees into his belly until he farted. She also tried it on me (when I got fussy).

When Aedan was a few weeks old, as I fed him on the couch in the middle of the night, I sat him up to burp. He proceeded to projectile vomit, exorcist style, from one end of the couch to the other—and beyond. He spray-painted the front door. The total carry distance had to have been twelve feet. Vomit would have gone farther if the door hadn't been shut.

From that point on, we tried to avoid wearing nice clothes when we fed or changed a baby, which meant that we never wore nice clothes. Burp cloths only provided the illusion of protection. Like many things in Reality—speeding, cheating on a spouse, avoiding taxes—we knew it was just a matter of time before we'd get caught.

In the best-case scenarios, our burp cloths got soaked but prevented chunks from landing on our shoulders. In the worst-case scenarios, we thought we had escaped all burp spew only to realize that people standing behind us could see a curdled mess running down the backs of our shirts. If the people near us grimaced but said nothing, we would realize our plight the instant we leaned against a chair's backrest. Cold and clammy, just like an ex-spouse.

Graduating to Solidish Foods

One of my great moments in parenting occurred when Aedan was about three-months old. He was on the floor and on his back, and he needed formula immediately. I threw together the bottle as quickly as I could, stuck it in his mouth, put his hands around it, and watched him feed *himself.* We still had to burp him, of course, but it was a small blessing to not have to hold him every time he needed to be fed.

Our boys graduated to a highchair when they were about six-months old. We also started giving them pureed food from a jar, including baby cereal. As conscientious parents, we followed some obligatory steps during this transitional period, such as tasting the baby food first. I wanted to know why the babies would sometimes devour the food and sometimes spit it out. Why was squash mixed with peas a big hit, but peas mixed with squash was a dud? When I could taste no difference, I considered other factors, such as boredom. With that hypothesis, I tried flying the spoon toward the child's mouth while making airplane noises. If that didn't work, I ate the baby food. Why waste it?

Once our kids had graduated to a highchair and pureed veggies, we became concerned about more than our clothing. What should we do about all the new "paint" on our walls and floors? Our dogs helped keep the floor and each other clean. They were willing to lick the babies clean too, but canine impulses to bathe babies did not set well with us. We stopped them when we could, for we knew those same dogs had recently removed detritus from my shoe.

Not willing to allow the dogs' assistance in bathing, we concluded that we would need to assume full responsibility for cleaning messes off our babies and walls. We always had a three-month supply of baby wipes on hand for mealtime. Wipes do a great job of cleaning babies and removing food from walls without damaging paint or wallpaper.

Preventative technologies are also available. I knew a family whose dad was some sort of engineer and he came up with a custom solution for feeding a baby. The device was like a mini wading pool with a hole cut in the middle. Parents could insert the baby through the hole, spread out the food in the wading pool, and let the baby "swim" in the food. When feeding time was over, the parents could simply remove the baby from the contraption and clean it in the sink.

Due to the awkwardness and impracticality of toting a wading pool with me, I preferred to carry a three-month supply of baby wipes, even when visiting my in-laws for just a few hours. Grandparents aren't used to having messes around the house, and I didn't want grandma to hyperventilate when pureed, semi-digested carrots sprayed across her new white carpet.

Our photo albums are full of pictures from that parenting era. Still today, we can tell what was for lunch based on the color of our sons' faces. Orange?

Pureed carrots. Green? Probably pureed pees. If yellow, squash. If our faces were sickly green, that meant Katie or I had gotten too close to the action or there had been a code brown.

Somewhere around eight or nine months of age, our babies got to eat finger food: finely chopped fruit, pasta, vegetables, and cheese. We knew it was time to experiment with finger food when the babies stared relentlessly at the food on our plates. By the time Brennan was age one, he would toddle over to me and demand that I give him food right off my plate.

We remembered our household Safety-First culture and perpetually watched for choking hazards and allergic reactions. We always remained nearby when our babies and toddlers ate. Nevertheless, when Aedan was about fifteen-months old, while he was overstuffing his face with Goldfish snacks, he began to choke. His face turned purple. That CPR class we took before he was born equipped me to save his life. I whacked Aedan on the back as I had been instructed and everything came up. After a terrifying thirty seconds, he could breathe again.

Other than everything I described in this chapter, feeding babies is fun. We had the privilege of being the people who had introduced our babies to a world of flavors. They'll be eating for the rest of their lives, but we'll always be the ones who started them on the culinary journey. We kept a camera nearby to document their faces when covered with chocolate cake on first birthdays. We plan on using those photos to embarrass them when they are adults, perhaps at their weddings, just like my parents did to me.

Bedtime

For parents, there is no greater time than bedtime. A sleeping baby is the most angelic thing in the world, and silence truly is golden. Adulting with Katie occurred in the magical hours after the babies had fallen asleep.

Adulting is crucial for parental sanity. We could drink a glass of wine uninterrupted, watch some TV, or (my personal favorite) play hide-the-pickle. Or we could fall asleep on the couch and, after an hour or two, drag ourselves to bed and wonder how we became so lame. What happened to those people who used to party until 2 a.m.?

Environment Is Key

From night one, we preferred our babies to sleep in a crib in their own rooms. Our strategy was to create an environment without many interruptions for us or the babies. For the nighttime routine, we bought Scout, a green, plush, programmable toy dog. We could customize Scout to do many things, including say our child's name, talk about his favorite color, sing lullabies and silly songs, and provide general entertainment.

Both boys loved their Scouts. By pushing buttons embedded in Scout's paws and stomach, they could get Scout to perform tricks. Our favorite was when Scout played lullaby music and put them to sleep. Scout also entertained the boys when they woke up too early in the morning. We still wonder if Scout brainwashed Aedan. We set Scout's favorite color to green, because Scout was a green dog. So, Scout repeatedly said to Aedan, "My favorite color is green, what's yours?" To this day Aedan's favorite color is green.

Like all parents, we were terrified of SIDS (sudden infant death syndrome). We bought a baby-monitor-and-sensor device. Placed under the crib mattress, the device would trigger an alarm on the monitor in our bedroom if the baby stopped moving. However, false alarms were not infrequent. Katie and I nearly had heart attacks when the device alarm went off in the middle of the night. We'd sprint down the hallway without touching the ground. In every case, the baby had curled up in a corner of the crib, causing the monitor to worry and thereby notify us. False alarms happened five times a month, but we figured it was still worth the peace of mind to keep using the device.

When we talked about having a third child, Katie worried about going through another pregnancy and all the associated woes. My main reason for not having a third child was interrupted sleep. I wasn't sure my heart could handle another round of alarms in the middle of the night. One study said it takes six years per kid for new parents to regain their quality of sleep. Did I really want to spend eighteen years without good sleep?

Bedtime Routines

Babies don't believe in set schedules. This is a problem in the modern world. They are too primal. When hungry, they eat. When tired, they sleep. When they need to poop or pee, they poop or pee. Tell a baby that 8 p.m. is bedtime and they respond with a blank look.

Nevertheless, Katie and I, being modern parents, studied prominent bedtime rituals. Some lasted hours. Some were simple, involving just a bottle, diaper change, and maybe some soothing music. Some were elaborate, similar to the Pope celebrating Easter Mass. All promised that, if followed religiously, the baby would fall asleep at the time designated by the parents.

We chose a straight-forward bedtime ritual that usually involved a bedtime bath. There is nothing like the smell of a clean baby. After the bath, we rubbed lavender-scented lotion all over the baby, applied the overnight diaper, and then threw on the pajamas. Next was to allow the baby to chugalug a bottle and, in the case of Aedan, let him do his football spike. When our sons were infants, we placed them in a sleep sack with Velcro straps. Swaddling seemed to help them feel comforted, as if they were still in the womb.

When they were a bit older, we would read Sandra Boyton's *The Going to Bed Book*. I can still remember the end, when the animals are on the ship and they "rock and rock and rock to sleep."

The book helped me go to bed too.

Infants can get flat spots on their heads unless the parents rotate their sleeping positions. We made sure that each baby's head was turned to the opposite end of the crib each night. (It took us a while to learn this trick, so Aedan developed a flat spot on his head. Thankfully, he grew out of it.) After the baby was positioned, we placed Scout in the crib, pressed his lullaby paw, slipped out of the room, and hoped for the best.

Despite our best efforts as modern parents, we sometimes failed. During the first three months, our babies had a tough time getting acclimated to a nighttime sleep schedule.

20:00   scheduled bedtime

21:15   baby falls asleep and mom calls it quits

22:30   dad goes to bed after drinking beer and watching sports

22:45   baby cries, so dad gets up to take care of the baby and to pee

00:00   baby falls asleep and dad gets back into bed

12:05   baby is awake and dad, because he must

work in the morning, insists it is mom's turn

01:30   baby finally sleeps and mom decides to sleep on the couch

04:30   baby needs a new diaper and a bottle; mom dozes while holding the bottle

05:15   baby goes back to sleep and mom thinks it is safe to go back to bed

06:00   alarm goes off and dad, with five hours of sleep, quietly gets ready for the workday but mom can't get back to sleep until he is gone

08:00   baby is up again

09:30   baby takes the first of his naps, which inclines mom to think briefly about taking a nap until she remembers that in Reality someone must do the laundry and dishes

11:30   baby needs a change, a bottle, and entertainment

Routines vary, depending on the family. Some couples we know like to sleep with their baby, which seems like a recipe for disaster. There could be an increased chance for a SIDS event or a reduced chance of everyone getting a good night's sleep. Other folks try the "cry it out" method. If the baby is fussy, they let the kid cry until he or she learns to "self-soothe." This is a test of wills that is tough for parents to win. Parents are programmed to take care of a crying baby. Our strategy was to see if the baby needed a diaper change or perhaps a bottle (based on the last feeding time). If those needs had been met, we would leave him with Scout. I think we got lucky, because we didn't have any prolonged, nightmarish, cry-for-hours events.

Naptime

Our best tool for imposing Aedan's daytime naps was a battery-powered swing. We'd set him in there, start it up, and he would conk out for a two-hour nap while rocking back and forth with the gentle beeps and bloops of lullaby music repeating endlessly until it became an earworm for any nearby adult.

Our second baby, Brennan, killed the swing. He was a big baby who grew rapidly. It was sad to see that little swing struggling to sway him back and forth. Brennan liked it, but we had to send the swing to an early retirement.

Our babies usually fell asleep during the five-minute car ride from the grocery store to home, which was awful. We would park the car, look in the review mirror, and see the child's scrunched up little face, eyes tightly shut, sleeping blissfully. Suddenly we were faced with two bad options.

Option A: Sit in the car while listening to the radio or while surfing the phone until the baby woke up, perhaps after a two-hour nap. If it was a hot day, the vehicle would get too warm, so starting the car and running the air conditioning was essential. This wasted gas for the next hour.

Option B: Try to be a ninja. Somehow open the car door without disturbing the baby. Then open the trunk to get the groceries. Now the driver's side door would be open, the trunk would be open, and I would be pretty sure I would wake the baby if I shut either one. Leaving them open would not be wise. So, upon shutting the doors, the baby would indeed wake up, and he would be fussy due to the rude interruption of his nap. After two hours of fussing at home, he would finally go to sleep again.

Sometimes our kids would snuggle up against

us and fall asleep when we were playing with them. That was cute as heck, especially when I was watching a football game, at least until I needed to pee. In those cases, I strengthened my ability to hold it, because to disturb a napping baby would f**k up the rest of the day.

Wherefore Art Thou?

I soon accepted a hard truth. My pre-baby life would never return. Whatever free time I had before my kids arrived had disappeared like special brownies at a hemp festival. Hanging out with friends? I had no time for friends anymore. My friends without kids couldn't relate to what I was going through anyway.

No one wants to be a recluse, so we tried to stay social. We sometimes took the pack-and-play to a friend's house and attempted to interact around a boardgame. In the best-case scenario, Aedan would fall asleep on time in an unfamiliar living room. In the worst-case scenario, he would demand constant attention thereby making the boardgame impossible to play.

We'd pay a price for staying up with friends

past midnight. Little boss didn't care that we were out late trying to be adults. After feedings and changings, Aedan would be up and ready to go at 6 a.m. We finally gave up and decided that sleep had to be a higher priority than having fun.

Entertainment

Here is a quick way to ruin a day: live with a bored baby or toddler. A bored baby will complain loudly and continuously. A bored toddler might burn down a house.

I Am the Entertainer

Babies don't only eat, sleep, and make messes in diapers. They are humans, so they require stimulation and interaction. I learned that to fulfill my role as a caregiver, I needed to develop new skills. I needed to become funny and interesting. My goal was stated by Billy Joel when he sang, "I am the entertainer, and I know just where I stand."

Babies appreciate a wide variety of games and activities. Mine gave me instant feedback about which they liked or didn't by either crying or smiling. My best performances generated laughter, which is one of the greatest feelings in the world. Laughter, I think, is a baby's way of saying "I love you."

The old classic games worked well and didn't require spending money. Peek-a-boo was always a hit with our boys. One study reported that peek-a-boo deludes babies into thinking that the adult has disappeared and suddenly reappeared, like magic. The trick only works for the first six months or so. After that babies understand "object permanence"; they know longer believe in disappearing and reappearing adults.

Making funny faces works well for most parents, but my face is scary. So, for me, blowing raspberries had a better outcome, even though I had to deal with the saliva on myself and the babies. As my sons got older, they learned they could blow raspberries on me. What goes around comes around.

Raspberries and other close-encounter games can be dangerous for parents. Our children grabbed necklaces, ears, and handfuls of hair. If our babies saw us react in pain, they would pull harder. I had to rescue Katie several times from a baby death grip on her hair. The more she screamed in agony, the more the kid pulled. A nice bounce on a knee was always fun. Unfortunately, Aedan had a habit of throwing his head backward. He cracked Katie on the nose more than once. He even threw his head back while just sitting in her lap, catching her completely unaware.

Self-Entertaining

For some reason, manufacturers think baby-safe versions of household items will interest babies. We had plastic keys, a fake TV remote that was *Sesame Street* themed, and a toy cellphone.

To save money, we dug out an old Xbox controller. I like to play video games and neither baby wanted to be left out. They were happy to mash some buttons or gnaw on the controller, all the while fascinated by the lights on the screen. Unfortunately, Aedan continued to put his mouth all over my controller and even destroyed the microphone on my gaming headset.

Once the babies could support their heads, we

introduced them to the jumparoo. The jumparoo was shaped like a flying saucer with a seat in the middle that hung down from three poles. It had some toys attached to the saucer, so when the baby stopped jumping, he still had something to occupy his time.

Aedan loved the jumparoo. He would bounce up and down as hard as he could for an hour, which was a great way to wear him out for the next nap. A quiet jumparoo often meant that Aedan had fallen asleep in the saucer, his head slumped off to the side.

Brennan loved the jumparoo too, until he broke it. On his first go around, he jumped twice and then, *ca-chunk!* A spring snapped. The toy had survived months of Aedan training in it like an Olympic athlete, but it could not survive three of Brennan's jumps.

Brennan grew faster than our hand-me-down toys could accommodate. The battery-powered swing failed him first, then the jumparoo. The next toy to fail was the walker. Built like me, Brennan couldn't fit his thighs through the leg holes in the seat. So, we bought an upgraded walker that was twice the price as the original and that had to be ordered online. It looked like a retro motorcycle complete with side mirrors, handlebars, lights, revving engine noises, music, and a built-in jumper. The vegan leather seat was larger to accommodate a bigger baby. Thus, it was the perfect match for Brennan. It was hilarious to see him bouncing, multitasking with the toys, and slamming into walls. It was less funny when he played bumper cars with our ankles. The dogs didn't like it either. A chubby little Dachshund can move fast when motivated.

Entertaining on the Road

Traveling with a baby was always a mixed bag. Katie often sat in the back seat with Aedan in case she needed to entertain him. On long trips, we hoped he would fall asleep. Sometimes Katie would fall asleep too and I'd be driving alone, fighting off the urge to take a nap. That always reminded me of the old joke: "I hope I die in my sleep like my grandfather, not crying in terror like the passengers in his car."

When Aedan was a baby, we packed a couple of toys, including Scout. The seat in front of him had a row of toys on it, but those never distracted him for long. We'd pack toys for Brennan, but he would inevitably bring his own toy and carry it with him all day, never letting go.

As our kids got a bit older, we would bring the Kindle and play a *Little Einsteins* episode. Aedan soon figured out how to use the touchscreen, enabling him to set up whatever entertainment he wanted. He liked playing the Angry Birds game, laughing hysterically as birds flew across the screen and crashed into pigs. As long as the battery didn't die before he fell asleep, we were fine.

Road trips were great until a boy dropped a deuce in a diaper. If Katie was riding in the back, she could swap the diaper while we were on the move. If she was sitting up front, we had to suffer with the stench until we could find a place to stop. For some reason, the smell never bothered the babies.

Self-Entertained Toddlers

Some have said that having a toddler is like being on a twenty-four-hour suicide watch. Suicide is no laughing matter, but I can't imagine a better description. Physically capable, but mentally immature little humans require constant attention, for the safety of everyone.

When Aedan first learned to walk, he developed a morning entertainment routine during which he wandered around the kitchen and family room opening cabinets, pulling heat vents up from the floor, trying to open the backdoor, and attempting to break through the baby gate. Then he'd settle down to watch *Little Einsteins*, probably in hopes of learning how to plot against us.

When Aedan got taller, he started reaching the countertops. He wasn't tall enough to see anything, so whatever he could reach he would pull off the counter. He managed to get cookies, plates, the mail, and other items. He once managed to reach the butcher block and pull out a long knife. Images of Chucky from the horror film *Child's Play* flashed through my mind. I don't know what your nightmares consist of, but mine now include a toddler wielding a knife. Fortunately, we got the knife from him without incident, and the butcher block was moved to a higher shelf.

To paraphrase former Secretary of Defense Donald Rumsfeld, there are a lot of "unknown unknowns." What's true for national defense is true for managing toddlers. Ours tested every limit of our Safety-First culture and revealed many unknown unknowns to us. Just when we thought our kids knew how to be safe on the stairs (so boring), they upped the danger level by hauling a ride-on toy to the top to see if they could slide down like Olympic bobsledders.

Brennan lost a front tooth before his fourth birthday. He was a physically active toddler who enjoyed couch climbing, spinning in circles, and attacking imaginary enemies with his ninjutsu powers in the hallway. We could never see the battle, but we could hear it as Brennan generated sound effects to accompany his kicking, hitting, and sword fighting. He shouted "Ninjago!" while charging through the house, ducking and weaving, diving to the ground, and getting pummeled by invisible forces that threw him against walls and furniture.

Brennan developed the habit of jumping from the second-lowest step straight to the marble floor. Even when we told him not to jump, he would do it anyway. Then, after sticking the landing like a pro gymnast, he'd tell us, "See? I'm fine." These words were usually followed by a dangerous stunt, likely involving a toy vehicle, a ramp, and a flaming hoop.

Electronic Coma

I got Aedan hooked on video games. He then convinced Katie to play with him while I was at work. The Lego video games are, in my opinion, perfect for a toddler, in part because violence is minimal. If a Lego guy dies, it just falls apart and then quickly reappears on the screen.

Aedan played so much Lego *Star Wars* that he unlocked every character available by amassing millions of Lego pips. One morning he started to delete the saved game file, which would reset his progress and lock him out of fifty characters. I warned him that he would regret it, but he said he wanted to start over and deleted the file anyway.

Sometimes all I could do was shrug and let him make a mistake. He never played enough of the game again to reopen the characters he had lost, even with Brennan's help. Now he regrets his decision. On the flip side, he no longer deletes any saved files. Sometimes I have to delete files to make room for new games.

Minecraft was even better than the Lego games. The boys could make themselves invincible and fly. They could have unlimited access to weapons or building blocks. With their imaginations to guide them, they could build and destroy for hours and hours. They enjoyed playing together, and I liked to join them too.

Disconnect

Katie and I didn't want our toddlers perpetually hooked up to electronics just to keep them out of our hair. We spent a lot of time figuring out other things for them to do.

We had physical *Star Wars*, Ninjago, and Minecraft Legos everywhere. This taught our kids the difference between the real world and the virtual world—sometimes the hard way. Even with a Safety-First culture at home, Aedan swallowed a Lego. He was eight, which means he should have known better. Katie told Aedan to notify her after every bowel movement. Baby poop smells bad, but big kid poop is foul indeed. Over the next few days, she grimaced while searching for the Lego in his poop with a plastic knife. Eventually she gave up the search. The lost Lego was never recovered. We assumed it passed safely.

Brennan never swallowed Legos, but he did get one stuck up his nose. It worked its way farther up and out of reach. We held the opposite nostril shut and had him blow, which shot the Lego out like a bullet. Stories about toddlers, Legos, and orifices seem to be ubiquitous.

Aedan had a brief fascination with little flying helicopters. During a two-year period, tiny drones and helicopters were all the rage. Granddad and I received several of them for Christmas. Aedan was so eager to fly those little toys that his hands got sweaty and trembled. They were not that easy to fly. Aedan would either fly them straight into a wall or, if we were outside, fly them out of the controller's range where they crashed to the ground. So, he required Granddad to fly his helicopters every time he came to visit. If Granddad didn't have the helicopters charged, or forgot them at home, the disappointment hung in the air like cheap cologne.

After the helicopter fad, it was balloons. Grandma bought a little helium tank so she could fill up balloons and if she left the tank at home, or ran out of helium, she had to deal with very disgruntled grandkids. She eventually bought *us* a tank of helium to keep the toddlers off *her* back.

We tried out some organized sports, but Aedan didn't like the cold weather and rain during soccer season. Ultimately, we decided to promote activities that would teach them skills that would be useful for a lifetime.

Aedan's first activity, at age three, was karate at the local dojo. That worked as well as you would expect for a kid with a lot of energy and the attention span of a fruit fly. After watching him tear around the room, disrupt the class, and ignore all directions from the instructors, the sensei asked us to come back in six months. Katie decided to wait a year. At age four, Aedan held it together and the sensei decided to work with him. By the time Brennan turned three, the dojo had created a new level of classes for the under-five crowd, most likely in response to Aedan and the challenges he presented at every class.

Swimming was next, when each boy turned three. In my opinion, every kid should learn to swim. It's a lifelong skill that might save a life, and it's fun and healthy.

A favorite activity for both kids occurred at the McDonalds play area. For our boys, it was also the answer to most of life's questions.

"Where do you boys want to eat?"

"McDonalds," they answered.

Other than Aedan's Egg McMuffin fetish, they weren't excited about the food. They just wanted to go to the play area.

"Good job passing your karate belt tests. What do you want for a reward?"

"McDonalds."

(When I was four, I would have asked for a He-Man toy.)

"We're going to go someplace you haven't been before. It will be fun."

"Where?" they asked.

"It's a surprise."

"I want to guess," Aedan said.

"Sure, go ahead."

"McDonalds."

"Didn't I say it was somewhere you haven't been before?"

"A different McDonalds," Aedan clarified.

Honestly, the folks at McDonalds are geniuses. If it weren't for the play area, we'd hardly eat there. But because of the play area, I took the boys regularly and therefore bought a plethora of McNuggets and McFlurries.

My goal as entertainer was simple: to give my boys experiences that I would want if I were a kid. If I'm lucky, they will grow up to be responsible adults with good jobs, becoming men who can take their dad golfing and fishing.

Mobility

Life changed again when Aedan decided to explore the world. I was at a work retreat the weekend it happened. He rolled over and then scooted forward on his belly, gaining confidence with every inch. Katie sent me a text message: "It's all over." Little did we know just how fun and challenging the next couple of years would be.

Aedan decided the army crawl was his preferred method of locomotion. He moved a lot faster than we could have imagined and his crawling style proved to be good practice for future karate class. Occasionally, he would experiment on his hands and knees, rocking back and forth but without going anywhere. When he was serious about moving, he would drop to his belly and crawl.

Brennan was a hands-and-knees guy, but he was never anxious to get anywhere. If he had toys around him, he was generally content to stay where he was. Food, however, motivated him. He would crawl to me, pull himself to his feet using my pants as leverage, open his mouth, and wait for me to feed him the food off my plate. This was cute at first, but less cute when he was older, at which point he would just take the plate and eat it all.

Babies have different ways of learning how to get around. Some prefer the butt scoot and others prefer the traditional hands-and-knees approach. Most learn the art of the roll early on, when they can flip from back to front. Some just keep rolling. Some like the bear crawl and some like the crab crawl. Aedan was quick to pull himself to his feet, first at a low windowsill and then on the couches, chairs, and fireplace hearth. Once he was on his feet, he learned to couch surf. All of this happened faster than we could mentally prepare.

Fear and Trembling

We were proud of our babies for their big advances in locomotion, but also rightfully terrified. Babies don't think about consequences and have no concept of danger. If a kid got hurt, we knew it would be our fault for failing to anticipate his next move or potential contact with household dangers. So, Katie and I crawled around on our hands and knees to see what a baby would see. We put bumpers on sharp furniture edges and secured cabinet doors and drawers. We vacuumed more frequently.

A mobile baby needs safe spaces. I once worried about a lost penny. Was it still on the floor somewhere? Dog toys, shoes, the dog's water bowl, the dog's food bowl—everything was a potential danger and had to be kept out of the baby's reach.

Cleaning under the recliner and couch was essential because a mobile baby could steal stuff and hide it there. If we lost our car keys, we checked under the couch. A dog frisbee went missing and we found it under the couch, along with two spoons.

Expensive or collectible items had to be moved to safe places, far out of reach of curious babies and toddlers. My collection of classic castle Lego sets from the eighties and nineties were moved from prominent displays on lower bookshelves, to shelves above the reach of a toddler standing on a chair.

Brennan still asks me when he will get the chance to play those Legos. My concern is his penchant for taking apart the minifigures, even removing their hands so that he can swap them for hands with other colors. He then creatively recombines the Lego sets to the point of unrecognizability. Eventually, all those pieces gather in a thirty-gallon bin where Minecraft meets Ninjago meets Marvel in a glorious mess that will never be properly sorted again. So, my answer to Brennan has been, "You'll inherit my Lego sets when I die."

Legos are just one type of danger to small children. Modern homes have other life-threatening hazards, such as electrical plugs and cords. We bought the electrical outlet covers and found ways to block the babies' access to other electrical items. Babies love to grab and tug on wires, including those attached to lamps. They might chew on cords attached to TVs, game systems, cheap surround sound systems, or that VCR player leftover from the Flintstones era. We had established a Safety-First culture in our home, so we used tape in less-than-elegant ways to secure the cords. We did not want to make a hospital trip.

Mobile babies can also be hazardous to adults. They are the second-most-dangerous creatures on earth. The only thing more dangerous is a toddler, which is what mobile babies aspire to be. For this reason, we considered hanging "Baby Crawling Here" signs on walls to avoid tripping over the little rug rats.

The dogs? Mobile babies are mortal threats to dogs. Ours hated the baby mobility phase. The babies loved grabbing dogs by the tails and ears. Aedan the army crawler once grabbed Cujo's tail and the dog dragged him a couple of feet, yipping the whole way. Of course, Cujo's yelps frightened Aedan, which made *him* cry, which led me to scold the poor dog, which I later felt guilty about.

We hooked Aedan up with the baby walker, which he figured out in a flash. Motoring down the hallway, he would multitask with toys while sucking on a pacifier. The dogs learned to stay clear due to Aedan's poor steering abilities. It was always full speed ahead until Aedan crashed into something.

They Toddle

At six months, Aedan was crawling. At seven months, he was couch surfing and using the walker.

At nine months, he was walking unaided. At twelve months, he was running—fast.

It was hard enough trying to protect crawling babies, but when they rose to their feet, we had to reexamine everything. Objects that had been high enough were no longer high enough. More bumpers were required for the newly accessible sharp edges. We put a lock on the oven and took the knobs off the stove. For a walking baby, stairs became a significant threat. A baby gate could stop a crawler, but a walking baby forced us to add security measures to gates near stairs. The job had to be done right: tight against the walls, a secure bar across the front.

Like a warden watching inmates, we kept an eye out for suspicious activity. We compared our boys to criminals serving life sentences: They were looking for a chance to break out and they thought they had nothing to lose. They watched us open and close the baby gate, observing how to operate the gate's mechanism. The little scamps even learned to climb over gates. We think they recruited our dogs to help them get out.

Just like toddlers, dogs don't like baby gates because they restrict dog freedom and limit access to food scraps. Thus, dogs share a common interest with toddlers, which leads them to become accomplices in child jailbreaks. Cujo got especially good at this. If we didn't set the baby gate perfectly, he could bump it with his nose and open it. Then we would hear the scurry of clawed feet and the patter of baby feet as the escapees charged through the house.

At thirteen months, Aedan climbed out of his crib. He was barely tall enough to see over the railing, so we didn't think he would be capable of breaking out. To our surprise, he somehow got his leg high enough to get a foot on the railing and was able to pull himself up and over. Therefore, we converted the crib to a toddler bed. Then Aedan could freely roam his room at night or during naptime. That was the end of the anti-SIDS alarm. We didn't want it going off every time Aedan decided to do a midnight walkabout. However, we still used the baby monitor with a camera. Katie would carry the handheld device with her everywhere during Aedan's naps, and it sat next to our bed at night. If he was up and moving around, we'd hear him or Scout.

Aedan used his climbing skills to get into everything. He climbed on countertops, on the backs of couches, and up the stairs. We taught him to slide down the stairs feet-first on his belly to keep from falling. He mastered the dining room table ascent, where he could grab at the chandelier. A fourteen-month-old kid might seem awkward and uncoordinated, but it was amazing to see how fast he could get into a bad situation. I once saw him sitting on a dining room chair eating yogurt and in a blink he was dancing on the table while spreading said yogurt all over the place with his feet. In that particular case, the dog was no help. Cujo the Dachshund, albeit longing for yogurt, scampered around the table in futility, cursing the day he was born with stubby legs.

Once, when Aedan was two, we put him down for a nap, waited an hour, and then entered the room only to realize that he was nowhere in sight. The door and window to his room had been kid proofed. There was no way he could have reached the latch, and he did not understand how to release it. As worry increased, we heard some banging from the built-in drawers under his bed. Then, slowly, one of them slid open. Aedan had managed to close the drawer while he was in it so he could take his nap in peace.

Mobile kids need a little privacy.

Fashion

The world of baby and toddler fashion is like a mix between the movie *Zoolander* and World Wrestling Entertainment. It can be outrageous like a pageant, or like a models' runway show, or just simple—throw on a diaper and let the kid run around like a barbarian.

Parental preferences for baby fashion are of little importance. We endured a barrage of pressure about clothing before our kids were born. Katie got a baby shower at work, one with my family on the West Coast, and one with her family on the East Coast. Bombarded with gifts, she received numerous outfits. These wardrobe additions came with the unspoken (and sometimes spoken) obligation to dress our babies in the clothes we had received and to somehow convey to the gift-giver how wonderful the clothing looked and how perfectly it fit . . . "or else." We are not sure what the "or else" meant, but such statements were certainly passive-aggressive.

As with all things baby, clothing needs change dramatically during the first few years. The situation progresses through stages of difficulty until the child can (hopefully) dress without help. Let us start with day one and go from there.

Baby Pageants

When Aedan was a newborn, we threw him into an article of clothing called a sleep sack. The bottom half of the outfit was the sack, which allowed him to freely kick within as needed. The upper part was a constrictive wrap. Some use the term *swaddle.* I called it a baby burrito. Terminology is not so important as function. The wrap was designed to hold his arms close to his body and to give him the simulated comfort of the womb. I've never seen scientific studies on comfort levels of babies in wombs; that said, I've seen sonogram images of babies in wombs, and those babies did not look comfortable. Whatever the case, someone came up with the idea that newborn babies would enjoy being in a burrito wrap. To complete the swaddle, we placed mittens on our kids' hands to prevent them from accidentally scratching their faces or eyes (when we freed their arms from the burrito wrap).

Sleep sacks did keep our boys warm at night. On cold nights we would increase the heat by throwing on a onesie before putting them in the sack. The downside? An overnight poop trapped inside a diaper, onesie, and a sleep sack would emit stench that could not escape into the atmosphere. Upon opening up all the layers, the smell would hit us like an Evander Holyfield haymaker.

I struggled to find motivation for dressing my babies after diaper changes. I knew I would be changing that diaper again very soon, sometimes within five minutes. So, putting clothes on the child seemed like a complete waste of time. I thought about leaving my babies naked except for a diaper. But we did not live in a tropical climate. I concluded that, without clothing, our boys would get cold. Then I thought about cranking up the thermostat. That idea evaporated when I considered paying exorbitant electric bills.

I also reasoned that leaving babies in diaper-only attire would leave me less protected in the event of a major blowout. Onesies can capture and absorb some overflowing poop, thereby limiting a sofa or carpet disaster.

On the other side of that coin, I reasoned that a diaper-only approach would spare Katie from the labor of cleaning poop-stained clothing. More than once Katie had looked at the results of a major blowout and decided to toss the clothes. Skid marks can be tough to get out of boxers but trying to get baby diarrhea out of a pair of baby pajamas can be a lost cause.

To further complicate my reasoning, I wondered about all those outfits we had received at baby showers. If we didn't dress our babies in that clothing, we could face the fearful "or else" from those kind people who gave us the outfits. Then, I realized that I might not be able to remember who gave us which outfit. I have no capacity in my brain for this sort of thing, but thankfully Katie does. If Aunt Beulah was going to be at the next family gathering, then Katie knew we had to dress the baby in the blue and brown striped onesie with the matching solid brown pants with the blue lion face on the butt. But since Grandma was going to be there, and she had just bought the baby a new outfit, we had to bring photo evidence (with a timestamp) that proved the baby had recently worn that gift.

The Advance of Time

Baby fashion is temporal. Babies arrive in non-uniform sizes and they grow fast. So, parents must fight an old nemesis: time. Aedan was bigger than most, so newborn clothes never fit him. Brennan was bigger than Aedan when he was born, but he ended up with mostly hand-me-downs.

Brennan's daily uniform for the first several years was a one piece, footed, zip-up pajama. Trying to fit a long-waisted, short-legged, large-for-his-age toddler in ill-fitting pajamas was like stuffing sausage into casing. If we used a larger size, the pajama legs were several inches too long and would bunch up around his ankles.

It might seem like Brennan got the short end of the stick, but he actually got to avoid a myriad of dress-up photo ops. At his first Thanksgiving, at age two months, Aedan had to dress as a pilgrim and pose for photos next to his three-month-old cousin. Neither kid could actually sit at that age;

instead, they leaned awkwardly on each other while reclining in a chair.

Then came the first Christmas when Aedan, along with five dogs belonging to the extended family, had to dress up in Christmas outfits: reindeer antlers for the dogs and a Santa hat for Aedan. I've had many hard jobs, but getting five dogs to wear reindeer antlers and to pose with a grumpy but clean-shaven three-month-old baby in a Santa hat is among the hardest. He had the rosy red cheeks, the chubby physique, and the twinkling eyes, but the non-verbal communication demonstrated zero Christmas cheer.

Football days presented us with new fashion dilemmas. On gamedays, Aedan was expected to don the uniform of two football teams. During the first game of the day, we would take a lot of pictures of Aedan in the uniform that represented the team of Aunt Beulah in Bothell. After the first game ended, we changed Aedan's uniform to honor Aunt Eunice's team in Philly.

Gameday shenanigans continued until Aedan was about six. Even at age nine, he told us in all seriousness that he rooted for the "Sea-gles," an amalgamation of his two grandmothers' football teams. We've tried to explain that he's supposed to root for two football teams on opposite coasts, but it hasn't sunk in yet.

Unlike adults, babies are easy-going when it comes to fashion. We could dress them any which way and they would never put up a fight. I like to think of them as action figures with occasional bouts of explosive diarrhea.

Toddlers on the other hand . . .

Are You Sure You Want to Wear That?

Once a tiny human learns to talk, she or he develops opinions and feelings. In Brennan's case, opinions and feelings were strongly linked to clothing. As soon as he could express his feelings, he wanted to choose his outfits.

As new parents, we learned that it was usually effective to give our toddlers a choice between two options. That gave the children an illusory feeling that they had power, which reduced conflict.

"Brennan, I told you to get your shorts on," I said, seeing that he was wearing sweats and a long-sleeve shirt. "It's almost eighty degrees outside."

"I like long sleeves down," Brennan replied, using his own vernacular to describe pants and long-sleeve shirts.

"It's too hot," I insisted. "If you're going to play outside you need shorts and a short-sleeve shirt." Then, feeling clever, I gave him a choice. "Would you rather wear your green shorts or the red ones with surfboards on them?"

"No thanks," he replied, attempting to end the conversation.

"That wasn't a 'no thanks' question," I remind him. "Green or red shorts?"

"No thanks."

I decided to get tough. "Either go change or you can't go outside."

"Okay, I'll stay inside," Brennan countered.

Now that my first attempts had failed, I had to become an authoritarian. "Go change into shorts and go outside, or you're losing privileges."

With a grumble, Brennan finally headed back to his room to do as he was told.

We repeated this scene at bedtime, before preschool in the mornings, on the way to every activity, and before every excursion to visit friends and relatives. I'm not sure why I had to keep telling Brennan to wear his karate *gi* like everyone else in his class, but I did.

Sometimes we gave up during clothing

conflicts, but with sarcasm. "Sure, wear your fluffy puppy pajamas with footies to bed tonight. The temperature in the house will be a cool seventy-eight degrees. You're not going to sweat at all."

"I'll be fine," Brennan assured us as he pulled the sheets and comforter over himself.

Brennan inherited Katie's grandfather's fashion sense. Popo was colorblind, which explained a lot. Brennan is not colorblind, but his idea of a coordinated outfit was similar to Popo's: red socks, green and white checkered shirt, navy blue pants, bright blue gloves, all accented with a white, red, and black hat. His inspiration for clothing selections could be best described as a leprechaun throwing up Lucky Charms cereal.

Aedan considered anything green worth wearing, when he was forced to wear *any* clothing. As a baby, he started kicking off his socks. As he became more coordinated, he learned how to take off all his clothes. Wearing nothing but a sagging diaper and a smile, Aedan would parade amuck through the house. That ended when Katie got pajamas that zipped up the back.

Aedan's tendency to wear nothing sometimes conflicted with formal occasions, those moments when he needed formal attire. At about age two, he wore a yellow and white striped seersucker shorts suit, bowtie, and coordinating fedora when he served as ringbearer in a wedding. Both brothers had nice outfits for Easter and other upscale occasions. However, we discovered that we could take the boy out of the jungle, but we could not take the jungle out of the boy.

One Easter, Aedan was wearing a cute pastel outfit that included: a crisp button-down shirt with light pink, baby blue, navy, and lime green plaid white background; pink bowtie; lime green V-neck argyle sweater vest; matching lime green argyle socks; khaki pants; and a woven baby-blue fedora. He had never worn such a perfectly coordinated outfit before . . . or since. It was a sunny day, but it had been raining nonstop the week prior. We had family over for brunch. When we went out to the patio for pictures in our Easter best, Aedan had his own ideas. He turned and ran as fast as his two-year-old legs could carry him. Unfortunately, they carried him to the pool.

Our pool had a cover designed to hold the weight of hundreds of gallons of rainwater. We had recently pumped water off the cover, but still some water remained. Aedan had been warned to stay off the cover, but that just inspired him to do the opposite. Horrified, Katie screamed at him to stop. Aedan charged onto the pool cover, falling into the puddle of dirty water that gathered around him. He then rolled around in the brown water and laughed hysterically.

None of the adults who ran after him wanted to step onto the cover to retrieve him. We waited. Thoroughly soaked, he eventually decided he had had his fun. He climbed out of the water and across the cover so I could lift him out.

Hand-Me-Way-Downs

Hand-me-down clothing is typical between siblings in most families, but my parents kept the clothes *I* wore as a kid. These ancient, sacred artifacts sat in boxes in my parents' garages for decades until I had my own home. Then my parents transferred the treasure to me.

I found the white suit I wore for a family portrait when I was two. There was the light blue Winnie the Pooh pajamas with worn-through footies and the Sherpa-lined suede vest. And next to that box of my forty-year-old clothing in the garage, there is a box of clothing that belonged to my boys when they were babies and toddlers. Eventually they will grow up and move away, and then one day I'll pass on the sacred artifacts to them. At that time, I'll make sure that I take pictures of my grandkids wearing my (by then) sixty-year-old clothing. And then those clothes can be packed away for the next generation.

Unfortunately, I never had Aedan and Brennan wear my childhood clothing for pictures or special occasions—a missed opportunity (at least for me).

Grandparents

Grandparents are funny creatures. In some families, they are the unsung heroes who raise the grandkids. Some are too far away to be involved except during the holidays. Some play the role of spoiler, giving grandkids candy and then sending them home hopped up on sugar.

When Katie and I got married, our parents asked: "When are you having a kid?" Katie was always offended by the question. She felt that everyone saw her only as a babymaker who was good for nothing else. I understood how she felt, but I tried to give her some perspective, reminding her that our parents wanted to be grandparents because they wanted the joy of having a kid around without the associated work. I reminded her that we would probably do the same thing to our boys.

Grandchildren love grandparents. The relationship is well illustrated on those tee-shirts that say: "Mom said no? Dial 1-800-Grandma." Grandparents have things that parents usually lack: time, money, and patience combined with a willingness to dole out ice cream. They also don't have to manage the fallout of saying yes to every childhood request, or the stress of having a little leech sucking out a parent's lifeforce.

As a result of this unfair situation, parents often feel jealous toward the grandparents of their children. When our sons were born, I started feeling a little resentful. My dad used to be interested in me, but now that I had kids, he often called to see if they could go fishing with him. What was I, chopped liver? But I normally suppressed my jealousy and gave him the OK, sometimes by inventing an excuse.

"Feel free to take the kids. It's Tuesday anyway, so I have to work."

"It's Tuesday? I thought it was Friday," Dad replied.

Must be nice to be retired.

Grandparents have a big advantage called "time on their hands." Parents, by contrast, have many conflicting priorities, such as working, cleaning house, buying groceries, and making food for the kids. I even burned a few days of vacation when the kids brought home a disgusting disease from school that bounced around our family for a week. I said goodbye to the paid days off I had planned to use during summer vacation.

However, grandparents can be highly selective about *when* they spend their free time with grandchildren. In our experience, grandparents believe that grandchildren are better after they have aged a few years, like a good cheese. I suppose they should know, because they have already survived babies and toddlers. This means they cannot be bamboozled. We tried to hoodwink our parents into babysitting by saying, "It has been *so easy* these past few months to care for Aedan." But they easily recognized the haggard look on our faces. They just smiled and repeated what they had said when I was a kid: "I hope you have a child just like you."

Grandparents are specialists at avoiding the unpleasant aspects of baby care. For example, Grandmom loved to hold baby Aedan during family gatherings. They had a great time, with Grandmom making faces and Aedan laughing.

But on more than one occasion, Grandmom would notice a foul smell. "Did you do that?" she would ask Aedan in a singsong voice. "Did you fart? That was soooo stinky."

Then, when the smell lingered too long, Grandmom would arise from the couch and wander the house with Aedan in her arms desperately looking for Katie. Everywhere she walked, she left a trail of stink behind, causing everyone to recoil in horror. Eventually Grandmom would find Katie.

"He needs a diaper change," Grandmom would say, handing Aedan over.

"Don't you know how to change a diaper?" Mama would ask.

"I don't do diapers," Grandmom would reply as she retreated to another part of the house.

As for grandfathers, they hide in garages, barns, sheds, or whatever structure they can find to avoid children with poopy diapers.

Reluctant Babysitters

I thought that having Grandmom live with us for several months a year and having Granddad and Grandma live close by would give us topnotch babysitting services at low rates. But we discovered that grandparents are the not-so-fast type of humans. If Katie and I wanted a date night, and if we wanted to leave the boys with the grandparents, we would need to endure an interrogation not unlike those faced by a teenage boy when he shows up to take an Army general's daughter on a date.

"Where are you going?"

"Are you going to make any other stops?"

"Who are you going to be with?"

"When are you going to get back?"

"Your cell phone is going to be on, right?"

"When was he last changed?"

"When was he last fed?"

Such questions from the grandparents represented a weak effort to pretend they had never taken care of a baby or toddler before. That way they couldn't be held responsible. Or perhaps they wanted to portray themselves as incompetent so that Katie and I wouldn't ask them to babysit too often. We learned quickly to disregard this strategy. Our parents clearly knew what was expected of them, and they were competent. They just didn't want to relive the nightmares of raising us—crying babies and exploding diapers.

However, in my view, our parents were too worried about babysitting our kids. Perhaps they did not realize that diaper technology had improved, that they would no longer need to use cloth diapers like my mom had to use on me. To get poop off my diapers, she had to soak them in a toilet before she could put them in the washing machine.

Nevertheless, our parents remained reluctant babysitters. When Aedan was eight and Brennan five, Katie and I needed to take some branches and garbage to the dump. We only needed forty-five minutes to complete the task, and our kids could practically take care of themselves. So, Katie asked Grandmom, who was playing solitaire on her computer, to briefly keep an eye on the kids.

Grandmom replied, "Don't stop for beers on the way back."

Katie was pissed. I, wanting to avoid conflict, assured my wife that her mother's statement was just a joke. Katie wasn't so sure.

Grandparents love to see the grandkids and do fun things. They just don't want to do the dirty work. So, knowing that our parents deeply loved our kids, I decided to use that knowledge to leverage free air conditioning repairs. My dad (Granddad) had built a forty-year career as an HVAC (heating, ventilation, and air conditioning) mechanic. Once, when our air conditioning went out during summer's ninety-degree days, I asked him to install a new one as a favor. He said something like, "My family rate is $50 per hour."

"You like your grandkids, right?" I asked.

"I *love* my grandkids," Granddad replied.

"You like being able to see them, right?"

"Right."

"And you don't want them to be stuck in hot house, do you?"

"I'll be right over with my tools," he grumbled. "But I'm doing it for their sake, not yours."

Comments like that made us wonder if we still mattered. My parents often said things like, "We'd love to see the boys. Oh, and you too." The boys were "the show" and I was just a grumpy, middle-age dude on his way to being a grumpy old dude.

Despite the push and pull, the grandparents agreed to watch Aedan overnight on a semi-regular basis. But when Brennan arrived, no one wanted to take responsibility for a three-year-old *and* a baby.

So, date nights turned into logistical nightmares. The thought of getting out of town for a couple of nights to celebrate our wedding anniversary seemed ludicrous, about as complex as working out the merger between AOL and Time Warner.

We miraculously lined up a trip without the kids. To make life easier for the grandparents, we split the kids between them. We updated some legal paperwork. One document was titled "Authorization of Medical Care." Signing it allowed the grandparents to make medical care decisions related to the boys if we were unavailable. We also updated our will in case we died (or ran off to Mexico). To leave five-month-old Brennan with my parents, Katie created a detailed list of feeding instructions. If his cheeks got red, use cream A. If his butt got red, use cream B. If his head got scaly, use cream C.

The stars aligned. We made it to Vegas for our fifth wedding anniversary. Everyone survived the experience. All joking aside, grandparents are a blessing.

Pets

A new baby doesn't mean pets are doomed, but when Aedan arrived, the quality of life for our two dogs—Cujo the Dachshund and Foster the Australian Shepard—took a turn for the worse.

Foster: Australian for Beer

Foster was an elderly eleven when Aedan was born. He weighed around forty pounds. His long legs made him look like a deer prancing through the woods. In his youth, he was extremely fast. He loved chasing frisbees and bringing them back. He'd play fetch for hours. In his later years, he wore out after a dozen tosses.

Foster, who was named after a beer, had a great life. If he had an online dating profile, he probably would have scored a bunch of dates. Katie had rescued him from a shelter while she was in college and living in a sorority. Foster became the mascot. (I wish I could have been a sorority mascot.) If Foster could have talked, I'm sure he could have told some great stories.

He got to travel too, moving with Katie from place to place throughout her twenties. He was born in Washington state, moved to New Jersey, Virginia, Washington, DC, and ultimately back to Washington state. He liked hikes and long walks on the beach.

We once had Foster's DNA tested to see what sort of mixed breed he was. We discovered that in addition to Australian Shepherd, he had Saluki, German Shepard, and Poodle DNA. His long legs, which looked like stilts, came from the Saluki lineage.

Cujo

As mentioned earlier, Cujo was a miniature Dachshund, weighing between thirteen and seventeen pounds, depending on the time of year. His weight changed seasonally because he would gorge on apples every fall and winter as apples fell off trees. The fattening process would go on for weeks. He possibly got drunk as the apples fermented. He would become thinner during spring and summer and then repeat the process in the fall.

Prior to Aedan's birth, Cujo was everyone's lap baby. When we visited friends and family, he always found someone willing to hold him. When he wasn't on a lap, he liked to play fetch with one, and only one, toy: a small green alien with feet. The green alien was so precious to him, that when we put it on top of the fridge to keep it out of Aedan's reach, Cujo would stare at the top of the fridge, eyes unblinking, until tears ran down his face.

The impact of Aedan's arrival hit Cujo hard. Foster had already been displaced by Cujo years before, so getting kicked down another rung on the ladder didn't seem to faze him. As long as Foster got his frisbee time, he was happy.

Cujo the lap dog, however, soon realized that he would have fewer lap opportunities. He preferred Katie's lap, but suddenly a baby usually occupied that spot. He couldn't compete. I'd put him in my lap, but he'd wander across the couch to see if he could get on Katie's. The "No Vacancy" sign was usually lit. As Aedan grew, Cujo had an even harder time getting into Katie's lap. If he wandered too close, Aedan often grabbed a handful of Cujo's hair.

The next decline in Cujo's life occurred when his beloved little green alien toy disappeared. We never found it. We bought similar green toys, and we tried a small blue alien with feet, but Cujo never played fetch again or showed attachment to any toys. The missing green alien is a mystery that will never be solved.

On the positive side, Cujo and Foster were best friends. Cujo always curled up on the bed with Foster. They were the odd couple, with a massive size difference. Despite being smaller, Cujo exerted his dominance and Foster didn't mind. Although Cujo had been displaced by a baby, he still had some authority and a friend to comfort him.

The dogs faced new challenges as Aedan became more mobile. Foster and Aedan usually ignored each other. Unfortunately, Cujo was not big enough to hold his own against Aedan, who once swung the poor dog around by the tail. Brennan committed minor infractions, like tail pulling and ear grabbing, but he learned how to be gentle with the dogs.

When Aedan was almost five and Brennan almost two, we had to put Foster down. He had lived nearly sixteen years. (Dogs grow old and die too fast.) It was our boys' first experience with death, but they seemed to process it well.

Cujo suffered the most when Foster died. Foster had been his close companion, and now Cujo was, in effect, alone. We gave Cujo plenty of attention, but the rest of his life was miserable.

Tucker

We decided to get a puppy about a year after Foster passed. We needed a breed that could put up with two young boys. We wanted the dog to be big, but not massive, and we hoped he could be a good companion for Cujo. So, we chose a Golden Retriever and named him Tucker.

Tucker was the right dog for our boys. Quickly growing to fifty-five pounds, he was rough and tough. He enjoyed wrestling, being chased, playing tug of war, and catching frisbees. We hope he'll live long enough to see both kids off to college.

Tucker has gravitated to me. He follows me everywhere. He's been my companion at work, sitting at my feet under my desk while waiting for quitting time. Affable and friendly, he insists on getting attention from everyone. We trained him to gently take treats, so he doesn't remove our fingers when snatching a morsel.

That he sticks with me like glue significantly reduces my privacy. When I'm at home with just family, I've never felt the need to lock the bathroom door. Tucker forced me to reconsider that habit. There was nothing worse than trying to take a shit with an audience, even if the audience was a dog. Then, following Tucker's lead, Katie and both boys—all of them—began to crowd into the bathroom during my business. Perhaps my children, wife, and dog didn't want me to get too comfortable. Perhaps Katie was thinking, *Why are you sitting on the shitter when there is a lawn to mow?*

Therefore, I established a locked-door policy. In response, Tucker started placing his toy duck in front of the bathroom door. Then he would walk about ten feet down the hallway and wait for me to come out. Exiting the bathroom, I would usually step on the duck, setting off the squeaker. Tucker would then bounce over, pick up the duck, and parade around my legs with it in his mouth.

As I write, Tucker is two feet behind my chair, waiting for me to get up so he can play a second round of frisbee. For a dog with tremendous energy, he has reservoirs of patience.

Choose Wisely

Cujo was eleven when we brought Tucker home. You could tell that Cujo had a *hell no* attitude about being displaced by another dog. He did not like Tucker from day one and let him know it. Within weeks, Tucker was as big as Cujo and within months he was double and then triple Cujo's size.

We soon had a dog personality mismatch in our home. Dachshunds are a take-no-crap breed and Cujo expected to be the boss. Foster was okay with that scenario, but Tucker had no intention of being pushed around. We weren't sure how to resolve it.

About a year later, Cujo got sick and died. His passing hit the boys hard, in part because they were older (four and seven). They still carry the hard experience of losing an animal.

I didn't expect to write such a grim story, but Cujo's last years were not too happy. No one planned that to happen. He just ended up being a mismatch for our growing family. The loss of Foster and the arrival of Tucker made his life even harder.

As we saw Cujo's plight, we wondered about finding someone without kids who might want him. But it didn't seem right to take him away from Foster, and we loved him. So we put that idea on the back burner. After Foster died, we talked again about rehoming Cujo, but decided that the kids, being older, would not tease him as much. We also knew that few people would be interested in a ten-year-old dog. Whatever the case, I doubt that rehoming him would have extended his life. We just regret that our family outgrew him. When we talk to young families who are thinking about adding a pet, we remember Cujo.

Toddler Diapers and Potty Training

A *baby's* diaper is, for the most part, a stationary target. Babies can wiggle and squirm and maybe crawl, but the parent can maintain full control. Changing a *toddler's* diaper is like trying to jump on a fast-moving train. As far as I know, no parent has died changing a toddler's diaper, but the smell and sight made us pray for death.

Our boys were (and still are) little barbarians. As toddlers, they preferred to be in diapers sans clothing while jumping, fighting invisible monsters, charging up and down stairs, and chasing the dogs. When they needed and even wanted a diaper change, they could not hold still long enough to let us change the diaper. So, we established a guiding principle for changing a toddler's diaper: Get it done ASAP.

Time Is of the Essence

To be more specific about the principle stated above, we stopped whatever we were doing and changed a diaper the instant we saw or smelled a problem. It did not matter what else was going on. We were proactive. If we had given the toddler a bottle, we changed the diaper within thirty minutes. If we forgot to do that, we paid the price later.

Urgency is essential because even the greatest diapers in the world, with all the new technology, can only hold so much pee and poop. So, when our toddler chugged eight ounces of formula and threw back a jar of pureed carrots and broccoli, the diaper would quickly give out. In our toddler-baby-and-two-dogs era, we often discovered pee puddles on the floor, despite making every effort to be proactive diaper changers.

We knew it was time to act fast when our boys' diapers sagged like a rapper's pants during a concert tour. The diaper would be hanging somewhere around the knees. At that point, we went into emergency pursuit mode. If it fell off before we could catch them, pee and/or poop could wind up anywhere (or everywhere).

With an active toddler, even solid poop (rare) will start leaking out within five minutes. Why? A diaper saturated with pee loses its ability to haul a load of poop. It will not seal well against a toddler's legs. Should the child choose to sit down, the dam will break.

Because diapers are flawed, we decided to respond to our failures with mercy. If we failed to act quickly, we chose to be merciful with ourselves. If we had just changed a diaper and within five minutes discovered that the toddler had filled up the new one, we were merciful. If the child failed to tell us about his need for a diaper, we were merciful. If the child knew we needed to change his diaper but decided to run away from us, we were merciful.

But we never understood why a toddler would want to carry around a load of crap in his pants. I certainly would not want that for myself, as evidenced by when I had a sneezing attack while needing to fart. Things turned out badly, and I experienced a tremendous urgency to resolve the outcome. But for some reason, our toddlers rarely worried about *sitting* in the outcome.

I say "rarely" because our kids sometimes took matters into their own hands, without waiting for us to change their diapers. Brennan decided, after pooping in his diaper, to toss it off the second-floor balcony. Poop splattered on an indoor plant, a throw rug, and a nearby wall. A year later, we rotated the plant to give the other side some sunlight and found dried poop on one of the leaves.

Aedan, during a backyard barbeque with friends, decided to pull his diaper down in front of everyone and poop on the lawn. It got worse. Cujo, who happened to be next to Aedan during the incident, decided to clean up the mess. Everyone at the barbecue, collectively and instinctively, shouted "No!" Cujo did not care what we thought.

Ah, memories!

To speed up urgent diaper changes, Katie wanted to engineer a "slap diaper" like the slap bracelets kids give out as party favors. Her proposed technology would enable Katie to grab the toddler, slow him down, get the old diaper off, wipe him, slap on the new diaper, and then release him to commit more household mayhem.

Even without slap technology, Katie was a pro at changing toddler diapers. She realized that changing tables no longer helped. With a toddler running around, she learned to improvise by imitating police arrest tactics. I frequently saw the boys facing the wall with hands up and legs spread while Katie swapped a dirty diaper.

I also saw her changing a diaper while a kid was on the move. She would follow behind him in a low crouch while juggling the new diaper, the old diaper, clean wipes, and dirty wipes. She could change diapers while the boys were strapped in car seats, on planes, and in public bathrooms. Her expertise came from hard work and practice. I estimated that she changed, on average, eight diapers per day . . . per kid . . . for four years . . . each. (Our kids were not quick to use the toilet.) That would amount to twenty-three thousand diapers.

Live and Learn

Aedan made nap time a challenge. We did our part to prepare, changing his diaper and putting on clean pajamas. But we could not stop him from pooping two-minutes after we'd left the room and, worse yet, we could not prevent him from removing his pajamas. Carnage followed. Lucky for me, I was at work during most nap-time events. I usually heard about them via texted pictures and vomiting emojis sent by Katie.

As she realizes now, her daily life for a solid six years, between the kids and aging dogs, mostly involved managing poop and vomit. Aedan recognized her misery. His early words included *eeew, gross,* and *yuck.* His vocabulary developed as he watched Katie cleaning up yet another mess.

For years, she had a strong stomach for cleaning up dog crap, but with the dogs and the kids both creating biological hazards in the house, she began to gag her way through every clean up. The really bad scenes even made *her* throw up. Aedan once decided to practice finger-painting with poop on the walls. Another time he pulled out some of the built-in bed drawers, squatted in them, pooped, and then shut the drawers. Katie had to clean out three separate drawers that day.

While I was at work, my phone would buzz when Katie sent me pictures from home. I'd take a quick peek to see what nightmare was unfolding. I would consider calling her to offer moral support, but I could not provide tangible help and I knew I'd lose a half hour of work while she chewed my ear off. It was best to let her unload on me when I got home.

Finger-painting on the wall is easy to spot. Other disaster signals were nebulous, such as subtle odors that couldn't be located in a room. Just a fart? Perhaps a lingering odor from a recently changed diaper? When this occurred, we decided it would be best to hunt for the odor's source. We once found poop mixed with mega blocks down a heating vent. While digging the blocks out of the vent, I found a brown one. That was a good lesson: Paranoia is healthy when a toddler's parent must stick an arm down a dark hole.

Potty Training

Katie and I finally decided that we were *done* with diapers, so we embraced the adventure of potty training. What could be better than a life without diapers and the joy of seeing a kid attend to his own bodily functions while sitting on an actual toilet? That would be like finding the Holy Grail. We knew that all kids eventually learned to use a toilet, so ours could too.

However, our boys lacked motivation. Aedan figured out that going to the bathroom, taking down his pull-ups, peeing, pulling up the pull-ups, and then washing his hands consumed a lot more time than getting a diaper changed. With the latter approach, he didn't even have to stop playing. He could stand at the couch with a couple of toys and entertain himself while Katie changed his diaper. Brennan had a similar perspective.

Apathy led to another issue. Both kids often "forgot" to inform us that they needed to pee or poop. We tried to get ahead of them by having them sit on the training potty at random intervals. Aedan didn't like the idea of peeing into the training potty. Sitting still was a challenge, and the idea of open-air peeing didn't appeal to him at all.

Brennan didn't mind sitting on the potty, especially if he could watch some cartoons from the little throne. (Yes, the potty sometimes hung out in the living room.) He would sit there for long stretches of time without a drop of pee. He once fell asleep on the pot while leaning forward against his Little Tikes Coupe.

Faced with these problems, we resorted to bribery. We told Aedan that we would give him Hot Wheels cars or Legos if he would tell us when he needed to go. That idea failed because delayed gratification was foreign to him. He wanted an instant reward every time he used the potty. We tried using his favorite snack: Goldfish crackers. That didn't motivate him; he wanted something out of the ordinary. Finally, the price was set with Skittles. Those did not produce a resounding success, but candy did move his motivation dial slightly in the right direction.

At this point, Aedan was almost four. We wanted to send him to preschool the next fall, but to be accepted he had to be fully potty trained. The other kids at preschool had finished potty training, but Aedan still had some hurdles to jump. The boys' pediatrician counseled patience. "You don't usually see teenagers in diapers," he said.

When he turned four, we made a clean break from daytime diapers, telling Aedan that he *had* to use the bathroom. We knew he had bladder control, because he had been holding his pee all night. He just needed motivation. After he peed in his underwear and pants a couple of times, he finally agreed to go to the bathroom when needed. Still, a typical trip to see the grandparents (a thirty-minute drive) went like this:

"Aedan, go to the bathroom before we leave."

"I don't need to go to the bathroom."

"You always say that. When was the last time you went?"

"I went earlier ago."

The phrase "earlier ago" could mean anything from one minute to millions of years. Toddlers have a very fluid and indeterminate grasp of time.

"Well, I want you to go now."

"I don't need to go."

That meant that there was no emergency, but that Aedan probably had a slight urge to pee. That left us with a choice: force him to go immediately or roll the dice during a thirty-minute car ride. Even when he was fully potty-trained, Aedan preferred rolling the dice. Most kids pee when they first wake up. Not this toddler. On many mornings, in the middle of breakfast, he would suddenly jump out of his chair and run to the nearest bathroom. He preferred bathroom emergencies because going to the bathroom took time away from more enjoyable activities.

Brennan was not an easier nut to crack than Aedan, but for different reasons. Whether learning to hold a bottle or learning to walk or learning to use the potty, Brennan was in no hurry. He did, however, want to feel like a big kid. To satisfy that need without actually making life changes, he decided to wear underwear *over* his diaper.

We tried bribing Brennan too. He was only willing to accept a bribe if it involved a lollipop. We felt he was too young for lollipops, but the troll (I mean toll) had to be paid. Due to our Safety-First household culture, we stipulated that Brennan could only eat a lollipop with adult supervision.

Eventually, Brennan got the hang of using the potty and graduated to only wearing overnight diapers. Shortly after he turned four, he was out of diapers completely. It was a good thing, because we had been special ordering overnight diapers that were big enough to fit him. If he had continued to resist, we would have had to give him small adult diapers.

We learned that we couldn't force potty training. Comparing our boys to other kids was not helpful. Nevertheless, bribery was worth the effort because successful potty training generated a household budget surplus. Using my estimate of twenty-three thousand diapers and seeing that the average price of a diaper was twenty cents, I concluded that the total cost of diapers for our two boys was $4,600.

Skittles and lollipops are a cheap price to pay to get toddler butts on the throne.

Feeding Toddlers

Compared to babies, toddlers need less parental attention when eating. Katie and I could put some finger food and a sippy cup with milk in front of them and let them go to town. To help them practice using utensils, we gave them a spoon and some applesauce or yogurt. Spoons, we learned, also make great catapults.

We could keep our toddlers confined in a highchair for a while. That limited the mess to nearby walls, floors, and humans. Our boys quickly came to dislike highchair confinement, preferring booster seats. This enabled them walk away from the table whenever they wanted. They preferred to eat and run, which is not a Safety-First practice and also generates food chaos. Our dogs helped clean up whatever hit the floor, which is why we referred to them as four-legged vacuums.

Dining Etiquette

Brennan had bad luck with Cujo. While sitting on a booster seat with, for example, a chicken nugget in his fist, Brennan would typically take a bite and then wave his hands or allow one hand to hang at his side. Cujo was always there, circling a like a hungry shark. If the chicken nugget came within striking distance, he would rip it out of Brennan's hands. Then there were tears.

This scene repeated many times because Brennan continued to forget to keep his food away from Cujo. Finally, by around age four, he started playing better defense, which was even more important now that we also had a fifty-five-pound Golden Retriever.

If the dogs didn't get food directly from a toddler, they always got food that randomly and constantly fell to the floor. Toddlers can't keep food on their plates. Trying to teach them this life skill is futile. Our boys liked to lean back in their chairs, wave the food around on the end of their forks, and let the gods decide what happened next. When food fell on the floor, they cried, even though we had just warned them to stop playing with the food. I always made extra food so I could head off the tears.

Due to the certain and widespread chaos generated by a toddler's meals, we carefully considered the relationship between clothing and types of food. A nice shirt and pants would be fine with crackers, but not with hot dogs and ketchup. We also concluded that a bib has little protective capacity. Dirty fingers get wiped on anything within reach, which means everything.

It feels like 90 percent of parenting a toddler involves repeating the same things for a thousand days. I was forced to bark a litany of daily orders.

"Use your napkin."

"Don't wipe your hands on your pants, or the chair, or your shirt."

"Don't wipe your face on your sleeves."

"Stop kicking each other under the table."

"Don't open your mouths and show each other your food; that's disgusting."

"Smaller bites, or you're going to choke."

"Don't you *dare* shove that whole thing in your mouth."

Rules for toddler table manners are pointless. Faces get wiped on sleeves. Hands get wiped on faces. Noses get wiped on parents. Everything gets wiped on dogs. (They don't mind.)

Electronic devices at the table gave us fits.

"Give me that Kindle," I said. "Mealtime is for talking to each other and enjoying the food; it's not for electronics."

"Why do I have to talk to other people?" asked Aedan.

This kid was willing to talk to every stranger he met, but he did not want to talk to us at the table. Already he thought that his parents were boring.

"It's good to know how to converse with people," I replied. "We should be talking to each other about our day. It's good practice for being an adult. Brennan, what did you do today?"

"Good," replied Brennan.

"I didn't ask you how your day was. I asked you what you did today."

Brennan mumbled something unintelligible. Aedan wolfed his food down and asked to be excused so he could play video games or watch Netflix.

"Great talk guys," I said as I wondered what went wrong with my parenting.

Even when they started showing signs of independence and could eat without help, we always hovered nearby and kept an eye on them. Both boys liked to shove massive quantities of food in their mouths. Aedan was the biggest offender, especially when it came to Goldfish crackers, which were his first love.

Katie had a conversation with Aedan at age two about Goldfish.

"I want Goldfish," Aedan said.

"The box is empty."

"Give me Goldfish."

"I can't sweetie. See? The box is empty." Katie showed Aedan the empty box.

"I want Goldfish."

Neither of us ever won an argument with a toddler. They should use toddlers to renegotiate trade tariffs with China. Toddlers know what they want, and they won't take no for an answer—even when the demand is impossible.

Abundant quantities of Goldfish were consumed in the family highchair, which sat in the same place in the kitchen for about five years, spanning our sons' toddler years. Despite regular cleaning, the wall behind the highchair got stained with a variety of food, spaghetti sauce being the worst. We eventually repainted the entire kitchen because there was no other way to get rid of the stains. I tried not to get teary while painting, for we were marking the end of an era, the era of children throwing food against the wall.

Healthy Choices

If the subheading above leads you to believe that I'm now going to write about proper preparation of locally sourced food, the relative pros and cons of GMO food, and how to replace cookies with apples, then I apologize for being misleading. To be clear, I'm going to write about the mental health of parents who feed toddlers.

Many parents search for the answer to an existential question: What will a toddler eat? The answer: Anything other than what the parents make. Only Goldfish is guaranteed to work. For Katie and I, that raised a practical question. Being good parents, we knew that our toddlers could not survive on Goldfish alone. They would need dietary variety.

So, Katie (usually) would spend forty-five minutes making white rice, sautéing vegetables in soy sauce, and crock-potting chicken breasts soaked in teriyaki. She would prepare the dish lovingly, cutting broccoli into Safety-First sizes, trimming fat off chicken, and making sure the toddler would only be served the most tender pre-cut morsels.

Her plating style wasn't perfect, but she would make the food look nice, especially for someone who lacked professional chef training. We would pour glasses of milk, set the placemats with forks, spoons, and napkins, and even dim the lights to set the mood.

The toddlers would usually be in a good mood, because they would have watched a marathon of "Mickey Mouse Clubhouse" while singing "hot dog, hot dog, hot diggity dog." We would tell them to turn the TV off, which would cause a few groans. But upon announcing the service of their dinner, the groans would turn to shouts of joy. The children would rush to the table, sit down, look at the plates, and one of them would say:

"What's this?"

"Chicken and rice with vegetables," Mama would reply.

"I don't like it."

"Yes, you do. I just made it last week and you ate all of it."

"I want a veggie pouch."

"Those are the same vegetables that are in the veggie pouch," I would say, in an effort to assist my wife.

Katie and I would see the toddler's cognitive wheels turning. Finally, the little boss would speak.

"I just want a veggie pouch."

"This is dinner," Mama would say. "You need to try it."

The toddler, feeling magnanimous, would agree to try a bite, but his face would be screwed up in disgust, even before he took the bite. He would smack his lips to emphasize that he was suffering while eating the chicken.

"I don't like it," he would announce, which did not surprise us.

"You're *going* to eat it," I would insist.

At this point, I would be growing short on patience and I would be comparing my toddler to the assholes at work, and I would be realizing that the toddler was slightly worse than them.

"I'd rather *die* than eat this." (Note: Actual toddler quote.) The toddler, at that point, would have thrown down the gauntlet.

"That can be arranged," I would say.

Obviously, I would never take out my toddler.

So, Katie and I developed options.

Option 1: Parental meltdown. Mama would perform, quite authentically, an emotional breakdown and cry. We hoped this would convince the toddler that he was being rude and needed to apologize. We hoped that he would realize that his mother had spent forty-five minutes making the food. We hoped that he would recognize the irrationality of preferring to die rather than eat his chicken. We hoped that he would acknowledge his mother's hard work on his behalf: changing diapers, doing laundry, cleaning dishes, and picking up toys throughout the house. Unfortunately, our toddler would often find it *funny* to see his mother cry.

Option 2: Bribery. We knew that toddlers enjoyed being bribed. The thought of getting candy or some other treat in exchange for eating dinner was a big win for them. They understood that they could draw a line in the sand and sometimes get what they wanted from a parent. They were not old enough to be politicians, but they already had all the *quid pro quo* skills they needed. So, the bribery method frequently worked, but not always.

"If you eat dinner you can have ice cream for dessert," I said.

"I want Goldfish," the toddler countered.

"Okay, if you eat dinner, you can have Goldfish," I replied, hoping to settle the matter without going to court.

The toddler, unready to give in, held up four fingers and said, "I want to take five bites of chicken, and then get Goldfish."

"That isn't the deal," I said. "Also, you only held up four fingers. If you're saying five, you have to hold up your whole hand."

I demonstrated for the toddler, but showed no signs of listening.

"Okay, seven bites." The toddler did not bother to hold up any fingers this time.

"No, you have to eat all of the dinner to get Goldfish."

"That isn't the deal," the toddler said, proving that the child *had actually been listening!*

Option 3: Threats. If options 1 and 2 failed, we would deploy threats, such as, "You can just *sit there* until you've eaten everything." Sometimes that threat worked, but our boys often sat there and played with the food, fork, spoon, napkin, and anything else within reach—for an hour. If the toddler sat there for an hour, then a Safety-First adult had to stay nearby for an hour, which amounted to the *adult's* punishment.

Now What?

Katie and I eventually learned that we needed to change tactics. We read somewhere that we should give toddlers two choices and let them pick. This method could be applied to any situation. Having a choice would give them a sense of power, and toddlers love power.

"You get to choose what you want to do," I said on one such occasion. "You can either eat all your food and get goldfish or you can *sit there* until you eat your food and not get goldfish. Your choice."

That was a lot of words, but the toddler clearly heard the Goldfish part.

"I want Goldfish."

I grabbed the Goldfish box from the cupboard and poured some into a bowl. "When you've finished eating all your food, you get this bowl."

The toddler agreed and began eating! I had succeeded in getting the toddler to eat! But the victory felt hollow. I had grown too tired to care that the toddler had only eaten half of his dinner before he grabbed the bowl of Goldfish. I rationalized my surrender. The toddler, after all, was a healthy little human, so fighting further about a bit of food no longer made sense.

Katie, also worn out, had left the table fifteen minutes earlier to hunt down a bottle of red wine. She found the bottle and decided to drink it in the living room, far from the toddler. She almost didn't bother getting a glass, but then she realized it would look undignified to chug wine out of the bottle, and she desired to raise a responsible adult, not a barbarian.

The toddling tyrant, sensing that he had almost vanquished his enemy, found a children's book and carried it over to his mother—along with the bowl of Goldfish. As he walked, Goldfish fell from the bowl and marked his trajectory. Cujo, recognizing Katie's limits and eager to help her, cleaned up the mess.

"Do you want me to read to you?" Katie asked.

"I've got it," I said. "Let's give Mama a break. It's 7:30, so we're going to read and then I'm putting you to bed."

Thankfully, the toddler did not argue against that idea or seek further negotiations. He seemed to think that it was profitable to occasionally allow his parents to have their way. We had all survived another day.

Dining Out

Parents, for some reason, think it is fun to take babies and toddlers to restaurants. Katie and I have never discovered that reason, but we *assumed* it would be joyful to introduce our babies to a wider variety of food by going to a restaurant. Brennan loved the spicy pickled coleslaw at a Mexican restaurant, as long as he could eat it straight from the bowl with his grubby hands. Due to the hot peppers in the slaw, the skin around his mouth would turn red. As for the chips, he just tossed them on the floor. Both of our boys were highly selective. They would devour whole beans, but if we gave them whole beans with rice, the rice ended up on the floor.

Every restaurant offers crayons and paper designed for children to develop artistic skills, but our toddlers preferred to drop the crayons onto the floor and then crawl underneath the table to retrieve them. Crawling on a restaurant floor is disgusting. The boys usually resurfaced with extra crayons, or a knife that had been under the seat for months, or a used napkin. They frequently shared observations about the difficulty of removing gum from the underside of the table.

So, I attempted to entertain Aedan at restaurants by teaching him to play tic-tac-toe. I played tic-tac-toe at every restaurant, a dozen times per visit, for years thereafter. Sometimes this tactic worked, but on one occasion, as Katie and I lost our appetites, one of our toddlers stood up and loudly announced to the entire restaurant: "I have to poop!"

Upon our departure, and admitting that our children had destroyed the environment, wasted food, and upset clients with shameless revelations about their intestinal functions, I always left a big tip.

Traveling

People might think that a kid at the grocery store is cute while he or she is commenting about "cawwots" and "pickoes" and "bwead" until the kid sees and elderly woman and yells, "Look, Mama! She's soooooo wiinkly!" Toddlers are basically frat boys at a bar, minus the booze.

Trips to the grocery store with kids are easy compared to long-distance journeys with kids. When traveling with our boys, Katie and I realized that we had become the people we disliked before we had kids.

Air Travel

When it came to pass that a long-distance trip would be necessary, Katie and I had to make some complicated decisions. First, while buying our plane tickets, we had to choose between keeping one heavy toddler on a parent's lap during a long flight or paying for an extra seat. The thought of having a big, fidgety toddler on a lap while confined to a small airplane seat usually compelled us to pay for the extra seat.

That created another problem: Airplanes often have only three seats together. This meant we would either need to place one kid into the care of a total stranger or leave one parent to manage two kids. Neither option was good. Katie and I once joked (sort of) about putting Aedan and Brennan side-by-side while we sat in another part of the plane. We dreamed of getting sloppy drunk together on the flight while a stranger managed our kids. We never acted on that dream. Instead, we would split up the family. I'd take one kid to one section of the plane and Katie would take the other kid to another section. Divide and conquer.

The next question was to decide who would be stuck with Brennan and his in-flight diaper changing needs, and who would be responsible for entertaining a hyperactive Aedan, who would certainly try to slip out of his seatbelt and run up and down the aisle. We usually flipped a coin to make that decision.

Then came the endless decisions about packing. It is impossible to pack light when traveling by air with babies and toddlers. They need booster seats and a car seats. They need sippy cups and bottles. They need diapers, stuffed animals, fully charged Kindles, dry snacks approved by Homeland Security, and entire wardrobes. Pre-travel packing questions gave us angst. Had we packed everything? Had we packed too much? Should we have shipped a box ahead?

Then came travel day logistics. Arriving at the airport, we would hook Brennan to a leash, the one we had previously used for Aedan. Yes, we kept our kid on a leash, like a dog. The parent assigned to Brennan would tie the other end of the leash to a belt loop. This allowed the parent to keep his or her hands free. Kid leashes are about survival, not dignity.

Katie somehow managed to get the bulk of our family clothing into one massive checked bag. To avoid paying too many bag fees, we would give Aedan a backpack and make him carry stuff like his Kindle and snacks. We would still have to carry the car seat on a collapsible frame with wheels, three backpacks, one carry-on bag, and a stroller in its own wheeled suitcase.

After checking the big bag and the stroller, we would then head to security while attempting to keep Aedan moving in the right direction while he played on his Kindle. TSA staff usually looked at us as if we were a collective threat; not a physical threat to the plane or the passengers, but a ruin-TSA-agents-day threat. To the chagrin of other passengers, TSA staff would yank us out of the normal line and move us to the precheck line, which, before we arrived, had been moving nicely.

Yes, we had liquids. We obviously could not bring a two-year-old on a five-hour plane ride without milk. Yes, TSA had to frisk us, and test the milk, and tear apart our car seats to ensure the absence of bombs.

"He drops his bombs in his diaper," I once unwisely joked. The TSA agent thought my joke was funny, but because I had said the word *bomb*, the agent now had to investigate the child's diaper. It was, of course, full of pee, but thankfully no bomb.

Now that we had been cleared by all thirty TSA agents, we could see that five hundred passengers in the traffic jam that *we had caused* were relieved to see us go, and they were praying that we would not be on their flights.

If we had time before our flight, we would stop at a restaurant in the terminal. After a game or two of tic-tac-toe with Aedan, we would head to the gate. Sometimes we would pass by an airport play area with a bunch of happy kids climbing on big toys and going down slides. Aedan always wanted to join them, but we would steer him away. Under no circumstances would we allow our kids to muck around in a germ-fest just before a two-week vacation. At the gate, the flight attendants would call for "people who need assistance and parents with little children." Being first on plane is one of the few advantages of traveling with babies and toddlers.

As I mentioned, Katie and I would flip a coin to see who got which kid. On one trip, I lost that coin toss. Katie ended up with Brennan. He needed the typical care: a bottle, a change, entertainment, and then a nap. He slept the entire five hours of the flight. Aedan, who was with me, wanted his Kindle right away. We had prepped the Kindle before we left. We had loaded up *Little Einsteins* videos, age-appropriate games, and a couple of Disney *Buddies* movies about Golden Retriever puppies. Aedan was set up for hours of entertainment. The plane seat even had a USB connection to recharge the battery.

I handed the Kindle to Aedan and then cued up

some music on my phone. I looked over to see what Aedan was doing on the Kindle and saw nothing but a message that said, "Confirm Factory Reset: Yes / No." Aedan hit the yes option before I could stop him.

Without an internet connection, there was nothing I could do. All of the information was saved in the cloud and I wasn't going to try to use plane's Wi-Fi to download full videos and movies. Suddenly it was all on me to entertain him.

We looked out the window and enjoyed the taxiing and takeoff. We loved the clouds and sky. Fifteen minutes later, we got bored. We had four hours and forty-five minutes to go. I gave him my phone and let him mess around with it. I took him to the bathroom. I gave him Goldfish and juice. I gave him my phone again, while ensuring that he didn't try to launch the factory reset. He eventually fell asleep with a couple of hours left and didn't wake up until we started the descent.

We had made it. No tantrums, few complaints, no major issues. Our seats were toward the front of the plane, so Aedan and I got off before Katie and Brennan. When they joined us, a passenger complimented us on our awesome job of flying with kids, adding that *we were great parents.*

Accolades like that weren't the norm. On the return flight of that same trip, Brennan sat next to Katie, laughing hard (screaming) with joy and happiness. The person sitting behind Katie was apparently unfamiliar with the sound of a happy baby and got up to say tersely in Katie's face, "Aren't you going to do something?"

"What? Why? He's happy. Would you rather I made him cry?"

On another trip, when Katie was flying alone with Aedan, he got sick on the descent, perhaps because he had consumed one too many bottles of formula during the flight. He threw up all over his seat. Katie used a bunch of wipes to clean it up as best she could. Then she changed Aedan's clothes while he sat in the seat. A flight attendant told her not to worry too much, adding that the airline would replace the seat when they landed. Kudos to the airline for being prepared. Perhaps Aedan's seat went to the incinerator.

Vehicle Travel

Every road trip, long or short, will have the same beginning: "Go to the bathroom before we leave." When our toddlers were still in diapers, we could skip that part, but when they were in potty training, we had to prepare for an incident on the road. Ours never admitted that they needed to pee or poop *before* a trip started; they waited until the car was on the freeway onramp.

When Katie and I embarked with the kids on a long trip, we always brought entertainment. Based on my highly scientific experiments with toddlers, adults can adequately entertain a toddler with conversation for about five minutes. Likewise, adults can only listen to about ten minutes of toddler complaints about being bored. After ten minutes, the risk of a parental stroke increases by 47 percent. To avoid the risk of stroke, it has been proven that adults should engage toddlers with other forms of entertainment.

In addition to entertainment, Katie and I found it helpful to offer the toddlers snacks, drinks, and clothing changes. The latter always came in handy, because our potty-training toddlers usually could not hold it until we reached a bathroom.

As previously stated, Katie and I operated with a Safety-First mindset. We always used one rule during vehicle travel: Never allow a toddler to access the driver. Nothing is more dangerous than a toddler with a projectile, long stick, or toy weapon in a moving car.

When Aedan drank a bottle of milk in the car, he would spike the bottle like he did at home. More than once his spike was horizontal rather than vertical, meaning the bottle was aimed at the back of my head while I was driving. I don't *think* he did this on purpose. Rather, my theory is that he, like all toddlers, lacked the ability to understand cause and effect.

Balloons from Red Robin were major dangers for us. Our kids loved eating at Red Robin, in part because they always got red balloons tied to plastic sticks. Need I say more about the subsequent drives? Before Brennan was born, Aedan struggled to suppress his urge to beat the balloons against the back of the driver's head. Once Brennan came along, the balloons became swords. He and Aedan would beat each other with them, taking an occasional swipe at Katie or me just to increase the adventure. Heaven forbid that a toddler's balloon should pop during a sword fight. In the world of toddler justice, the kid with the popped balloon would need to pop his brother's balloon. This reminded me of communist economics. If everyone suffers equally, life is good.

Katie and I also struggled to answer a major life question: At what age does it become the toddler's responsibility to remember to recharge his Kindle? We think the answer is relative. It depends on the desperation level of the parents and the estimated time of each road trip. In the case of a forty-five-minute car ride to visit the grandparents, Mama should make sure the Kindles are charged. In the case of a five-minute ride to preschool, the toddler should assume responsibility.

Turning on the car radio might seem like an easy entertainment solution, but Katie and I learned that pop stations are not safe for parroting toddlers. We realized that we could inadvertently teach our toddlers some highly advanced vocabulary. So we decided to play Disney music or let them watch *Duck Tales* or *Jake and the Neverland Pirates* or *Mickey Mouse Clubhouse*. When Katie and I started to sing Disney music, we recognized our need for a childless vacation. If we did not get a vacation without the kids our chances of needing professional help increased dramatically.

Linguistic Evolution

Covered in poop, pureed veggies, and baby vomit. Sleepless. Disney songs in our heads. Perpetually tempted to guzzle wine from the bottle. Despite those realities, Katie and I wouldn't have traded our kids for anything.

When they were infants, when they were sucking on a bottle with a sailor's vigor, we wondered what they were thinking. What were their hopes? Their dreams? We eagerly awaited the day when they could tell us, when they would say, "I love you." That would make it all worthwhile.

The first sounds from a baby are akin to babbling, a step forward from straight up crying and screaming. There are even some repetitive sounds, such as "ba-ba-ba." This advancement encouraged Katie to offer instruction to our baby.

"Ma-ma," she would say with extra enunciation. "Mama. Maaa-maaa. Mama." Nothing generated immediate results, despite daily lessons over the course of weeks.

Then, when I checked out the babbling baby, he suddenly, and without my encouragement, said "daaa-daaa."

And again, "dada."

My baby, *my son,* had said, "dada."

Katie rose to her feet and screamed, "Goddammit!" Then she contemplated how to strangle her husband.

It Speaks

By some coincidence of linguistic development, babbling babies usually say "dada" before "mama," even though dads usually spend less time with infants than mothers do. It doesn't seem fair that dad should get the bragging rights, but mothers should remember that babies don't know what they're saying.

I reminded Katie that, in a few months, the baby would soon pronounce "mama" and "dada" and know the difference between each person.

Then, over the next couple of years, the baby would learn a lot of new words. In fact, at times, Katie and I regretted our sons' abilities to speak. But I'm getting ahead of myself.

Katie started Aedan on baby sign language, teaching him simple signs for *milk* and *thank you*. He easily picked up the signs, so Katie quickly ran out of new signs to teach him. Aedan's sign language classes ended by the time we had Brennan.

Aedan had an interesting approach to words. He liked to eat strawberries, but he didn't like the word. So, he called them *dice* for a long time. He even poopooed the word *milk* and replaced it with *no*, which was confusing when rebellion and milk were simultaneously involved.

Toddler talk can be impossible to understand. We could understand about 80 percent what our kids said, and maybe 60 percent of what other toddlers said. So, I had to ask my kids to repeat themselves a lot. This often caused Brennan to become super frustrated with me. He'd yell "never mind!" and stomp away angrily. *That* I could understand perfectly.

It doesn't help that toddlers usually cry while they are talking. When one of our boys was trying to cry and talk at the same time, I let him know that I couldn't understand him. He frequently stopped crying so he could explain the problem.

Aedan pulled a trick when he was sitting in his highchair eating miniature raviolis. Katie had to step out of the room briefly. She returned to find that his food had disappeared. There was no way he could have eaten it all so quickly.

"Where'd your raviolis go?"

"They're hiding," Aedan replied.

"What do you mean they're hiding? Did you feed them to the dogs?"

"No."

"Where did they go?"

"They're hiding," Aedan insisted.

"I found the dish you threw in the sink. Where are the raviolis?"

"They're hiding."

We're pretty sure the raviolis were hiding in the dogs.

Brennan's first words were, predictably, *mama* and *dada*. Another of his first words was *Aedan*, because he had heard us say, with frequency, things like "Aedan! Leave the dogs alone!" or "Aedan! Go to time out!"

Katie once asked Aedan if he was hungry. He replied by saying, "I'm not hungry, I'm Aedan!" He wasn't joking. Humor was tough for our boys to grasp.

Our toddlers required numerous explanations to grasp simple truths. Katie had a long conversation with Aedan during which she tried to help him understand the difference between two uncles: my brother and the husband of Katie's sister. Katie explained each uncle's relationship to Aedan and then asked him, "Do you remember who my sister is?"

"Michael Jackson," Aedan replied.

We have no idea where that response came from. Even today, I don't think he would know who Michael Jackson was.

Now They Listen

Sometimes our kids could pick up exactly what we had said, know how to use it, and run into big trouble. Returning from the mall with Aedan in the car, another driver made an illegal right turn and almost T-boned us while I passed through an intersection. Fortunately, we escaped a bad accident, but in that emotional moment, I exclaimed: "What the f**king heck!" I immediately told Aedan, "Do not repeat that."

A few days later, Katie was driving with Aedan when another driver merged in front of her. When Katie hit the brakes, Aedan asked, "What are you doing?"

"A car pulled out in front of me. I slowed down so I wouldn't hit him. There are rules for driving. I have to obey the rules so we don't crash. If we crash and I am going too fast, the police would give me a ticket. Or if we got hurt, they would call the ambulance."

"Then they would say, 'What the f**king heck!'" Aedan added.

Weeks later, Katie taught Aedan what to do in an emergency.

"If there's a bad guy breaking in and you dial 911," she said, "what do you say?"

"What the f**king heck!!!" Aedan replied.

Obviously, my Parent of the Year award got lost in the mail.

After preschool one day, Katie asked Aedan about what he did in school.

"I was very good," Aedan said. "We learned all about dinosaurs today."

"Which dinosaurs?" Katie asked.

"T-rex."

"Which one was your favorite?"

"T-rex."

"Dinosaurs were big and scary. I'm glad they are all dead now."

"They're not dead," Aedan replied, slightly puzzled.

"Yes, they are," Katie explained. "They went extinct a long time ago."

"Ex-stinked . . . like a fart?"

"No, honey. They are all dead, or extinct."

"The dinosaurs are living in a zoo in Africa."

"No, Aedan, they are all dead."

"Mama! They are not dead! I'm so mad at you!!!!" Aedan howled.

Brennan frequently got angry at Katie. He learned some unique ways to express himself, and he let Katie know how he felt. A couple of years ago, Katie made him mad for some reason and he said, "Mama, I'm going to kick you in the butt!"

"What did you say!?"

"Mama. I'm going to kick you in the butt."

Brennan was either brave or not very smart. I can't claim credit for his quip. He didn't hear that line from me. I blamed the other kids at his preschool.

Even preschoolers get homework now. Brennan's

homework was simple: writing his name five times, cutting out pictures, coloring other pictures—fun stuff that develops motor skills. As Katie helped him one day work with scissors, Brennan said, "Now I don't have to get rid of you." Katie walked away, unsure of how to respond. We later asked Brennan how he planned to get rid of his mother.

"Throw her in the trash," he replied.

"I don't think she'll fit," I pointed out. Then he babbled about how his plan would work while punching and kicking the air.

Brennan recently threatened Katie again, while carrying his foam Minecraft sword. "Mama, if you don't do what I say, I'm going to sword you."

"Just who do you think you are?!"

"Brennan Houston."

Sometime soon I plan to recommend that Brennan reconsider how he speaks to Katie, for she is tougher than he thinks.

Budding Comedians?

Toddlers love to tell jokes, but they are terrible at it. If we laughed at our kids at the wrong time, they would get upset. And sometimes, they told hilarious jokes without knowing it. For example, Brennan one night had to pee about fifteen times in an hour. He complained that it hurt. I became concerned he might have a urinary tract infection, but it was 9 p.m. and I hoped that we could avoid the emergency room and hold on until the next morning.

He started to cry, saying, "My penis won't let me sleep."

I was sure that every guy could make that claim, albeit for different reasons.

I hit on an ingenious solution and gave him a diaper. Brennan was thrilled. He wore the diaper, slept through the night, and we went to the doctor the next morning.

At the doctor's visit, I let him explain the problem. He told the doctor that his penis wouldn't let him sleep. The doctor, like me, tried to suppress laughter, causing his face to turn a bit red. Eventually, he took a urine sample, gave us a prescription for antibiotics, and away we went.

I decided to teach Aedan some jokes when he was about three. Pete and Repeat jokes got old fast, so I started using knock-knock jokes. Those are the lowest form of humor. When toddlers try to make them up, they are horrible.

"Knock-knock," Aedan said.

"Who's there?" I asked.

"Spider-man."

"Spider-man who?"

"Spider-man going to kick you in the butt!"

At that moment, I realized that the preschool kids might not be the ones who had taught Brennan that "kick you in the butt" line. Then I told Aedan that his joke was not funny, but he disagreed with me. Humor is in the ear of the listener, I guess.

Brennan, knowing that Aedan could read well, and hoping to measure up, figured he would fake it until he could make it. During a car ride home from school, Brennan told Katie he knew how to read. Katie pointed to a carwash sign and asked him, "What does that sign say?" Brennan stuttered and stammered for a minute and then replied, "It says . . . uh, you can't read!"

He abandoned his pretense quickly, but he never lost his aspirations for life. When Brennan was four, the doctor once asked him what he wanted to be when he grew up. Brennan said, "Five." Despite his young age, I could see that he was setting incremental and achievable goals.

Discipline

This is the chapter every parent has been waiting for. It's one thing to spend all this time taking care of and coddling our little angels, but what does a parent do when that little angel turns into a horned little pyromaniac and lights the couch on fire? Thankfully, that didn't happen to us, but our children have caused Katie and I, at times, to seriously doubt our sanity.

Don't Let Them Break You

When Aedan was throwing his toys down our heating vents day after day and against every recrimination, I would ask, *Am I losing my mind? Is life worth living anymore? Am I a bad parent? Is there something seriously wrong with my child?*

Now that I'm more experienced, I've answered no to all of those questions. Babies and toddlers are risk takers, problem solvers, and limit pushers. They are designed that way. It helped me to imagine what it would be like to learn to walk. Suddenly babies have to embrace risk and fall a lot. They learn to pull themselves up on couches and chairs, and then they repeatedly fall after taking just a few steps. Trying again and again requires a tough attitude, and with that attitude they eventually turn halting steps into confident steps, and confident steps into running.

That attitude, later on, enabled Aedan to ride a bike without training wheels, even though it was a tough experience. His instincts worked against him. He knew that increased speed would make it hurt more if he crashed, but that without enough speed he would fall anyway. Finding that balance was difficult to learn. At first, he was too cautious.

As I came to understand that my babies and toddlers needed a risk-embracing attitude to grow and advance, I discovered that my job as father was simple: to survive and to make sure the kids survived.

Our boys have outgrown bad habits and formed

new ones. Brennan hasn't tossed any poopy diapers off the top balcony in years. Aedan doesn't use his built-in drawers for a toilet. Neither of them has used a crayon on the walls in a long time. Katie and I still exist. We have all survived.

My initial strategy with changing my children's bad habits was and continues to be repetition. By this I mean repeating the same commands and guidelines until the child finally comprehends and eventually grows out of his wrong behavior. Repeating these basic things is not exciting, but it gives the kids time to outgrow bad habits and it spares me from the need to deliver long lectures.

Sometimes our kids would listen and obey, but usually they would hear us say for the hundredth time, "Don't pull on the dog's tail," and then immediately pull the dog's tail until it yelped. It's normal at this point to become an angry parent. I still don't understand how a toddler could clearly and repeatedly hear what I told him not to do and then do the opposite. Either he couldn't comprehend the words, or he straight up wanted to test my authority.

Regardless, Katie and I knew that we could not let our kids get away with wrong behavior. Otherwise, what might they do later?

Discipline

Our initial go-to punishment for Aedan was a time-out. If needed, we would escalate punishments by removing electronics. However, Aedan found it difficult to grasp how the loss of his Kindle privileges "for the day" connected to his bad behavior. Why a whole day? Brennan, at age five, struggled to understand the difference between five minutes, five hours, five days, and five weeks.

The concept of what "today" means can be completely lost on toddlers. The solar system is no help, either. During the summer where we live, dawn begins at 4:30 a.m. and dusk occurs at about 10 p.m. Understandably, our boys found it difficult to understand why they had to go to bed at 8 p.m. when the sun was still high and bright. I tried to explain the tilt of the earth during summer versus winter. Sometimes, I talked about summer and winter in different hemispheres. I eventually gave up when the child's glassy eyes turned away in boredom.

By the time Brennan turned one, our time-out approach to discipline had become passé for Aedan. When a disciplinary method becomes passé, a kid is like a convict who gets out of jail after eleven years, violates parole, and ends back up in jail. At least in jail he gets "three hots and a cot."

Thus, the need for punishment escalation. Aedan eventually understood what it meant to lose his Kindle privileges for a day (or more). He finally understood that losing electronics was the *worst punishment ever.* He would have to play with his regular toys and interact with real people, especially his parents. It was good to have an effective method up our sleeve.

A punishment used in Aedan's karate class gave us another idea. When kids were late to practice, or didn't listen, or misbehaved, the instructors would stop class and tell the offender to do pushups while everyone watched. (As an aside, I thought the *parents* should do the pushups if the kid was late, but not being one to like pushups, I never voiced my opinion.)

So, at home, pushups quickly replaced time-out. Our typical maximum required number of pushups was twenty. They could be mandated almost everywhere, or they could be deferred until after a problematic car ride. Pushups helped our boys develop strong arms, especially as often as they needed to do them. We've dished out pushups in public, without hesitation. If one kid punched his brother, it was pushup time—even in six inches of snow. The crime was committed, the debt was paid immediately, and forgiveness quickly followed. Over and done.

Other parents, upon seeing our sons doing pushups, expressed admiration for our methodology. However, if there was a downside to pushups as a punishment, it was the boys' terrible form. I can tell you that, at young ages, the kids looked like they were trying to do the "worm." I can also tell you that their form was better than mine. My pushups looked like that commercial from the eighties when the old gal was on the floor shouting, "I've fallen, and I can't get up!"

We still remove electronics to punish the boys, but we've unintentionally parsed the electronics into so many categories that we've found it difficult to know when, if, and how long to ban certain items. For example, it was a terrible time to institute a total-electronics ban when I took both kids to karate class. I knew that I would need to keep a seven-year-old boy busy for forty-five minutes while his brother was in class and then keep a four-year-old boy busy for an hour while his brother was in class. Thus, my total-electronics bans had exceptions, including the Kindle and my phone, which led to the loss of *my* cell phone privileges.

Neither Katie nor I enjoyed punishing kids. We found no pleasure in telling them for the fifteenth time in five minutes to get their shoes on when heading to school. But if sixteen commands were needed for them to get their shoes on, we had to make them do ten pushups. We had to teach them how to follow rules and respect authority, or they might find the "justice" system doing it later. We did not want them to find out the hard way.

What's the Point?

Parents can easily get lost in the cycle of misbehavior and punishment. Katie and I often wondered if we were applying discipline correctly. Too severe? Too lenient? Were the kids learning real lessons for life? Would they resent us? In the midst of these questions, we wanted them to learn as much as they could while we still had maximum influence. To keep our eyes on the ball, we reminded ourselves and the boys that we needed to teach them self-discipline. They would need that to be responsible adults.

As often as we used punishments to deter undesirable behaviors, we also used rewards to encourage good behaviors. Unfortunately, the line between discouraging bad behaviors and encouraging good ones is often blurry. For example, in preschool, both kids started getting homework. I believed they should finish their homework the instant they got home from school, which would maximize their free time. If they stayed focused, the homework wouldn't take them more than a few minutes.

However, instead of sitting down and completing the homework, the boys would cry, falsely claiming, "I never have time to play." They tried to redirect the issue, saying, "I'm hungry." If I turned my back, they would flee to another part of the house and force me to hunt them down. This turned a ten-minute homework activity into a two-hour ordeal.

We tried mild threats: "Do your homework now, or you'll lose video game privileges. Your choice." We tried bribery: "Finish your homework and I'll give you a cookie." We tried logic: "If you don't complain and just get your homework done, you'll have more time to play." Sometimes one of these approaches worked. Sometimes none of them worked. But, importantly, Katie and I tried to remember that our goal was to get them to do homework without being asked. We wanted to instill self-discipline!

Since preschool, teachers had graded our boys on behavior, using three categories. Instead of letter grades, a traffic light system was used. Red was bad and green was good. The kids knew they had a good day in class when they got three greens. At home, we always asked what they got on their behavior charts. They understood that getting reds might involve additional punishments at home, especially on those rare three-red-light days.

We also promised rewards if the boys got fifteen greens in a week. I once rewarded Aedan by taking him to play laser tag. Two months later, Aedan received an assignment to write a narrative in the first person about an interesting or important activity. He wrote about playing laser tag with me. He included details that I didn't consider important, but that had impacted him.

During the first game, he killed me more than I killed him. (I intentionally avoided shooting him.) He was proud of beating me until he realized that I had come in second out of fifteen people and that he had come in twelfth. Seeing that I was good at this game, he wanted to team up with me. In the second game, playing as a father-son team, I came in second out of eighteen and Aedan came in twelfth again. Because more people were playing, he had improved.

My point is this: Two months after we played laser tag, he still remembered our time together and wrote it all down. It was a huge deal for him and reminded me that everything we do with our kids can stick. As parents, all we can do is keep trying and hope for the best.

Sharpen the Saw

Regardless of the circumstances, parents must sharpen the saw.

I borrowed this analogy from Stephen R. Covey's book *7 Habits of Highly Successful People*. It helped me kickstart my attempt at self-reflection. I highly recommend the book, which I have read multiple times.

"Sharpening the Saw" is one of Covey's seven habits. According to Covey, there are four aspects of life to sharpen: physical, social/emotional, mental, and spiritual. A sharp saw in each area will "cut wood" better than a dull one. So, to be the best parent I can be, I need to sharpen my parenting saw. To do that, I need to stop cutting wood.

How Quickly We Forget

Children require a lot of care. A stay-at-home parent rarely gets a break. The baby is either sleeping or clinging to the parent (or both at the same time). It becomes hard to differentiate between where the baby ends and the parent begins. That makes it easy for parents to neglect self-care.

Parents who work outside the home all day come home tired and look forward to having a beer or three. But working parents need time with their babies. Dishes and laundry must get done. There is the yard work. Other demands perpetually peck at us. With babies around, parents can't use evenings and weekends to recharge. Life is fully occupied by the tiny lives we brought into the world.

I remember who I used to be. Dancing, nachos and a beer after work while watching Monday Night Football, a video game with a buddy—that person still exists. That person needs a chance to live.

Katie and I knew that having a baby would be long-term commitment. We knew life would change. We adapted and did everything we could to make it work. We put everything else on the back burner in the struggle for daily survival. But we had to sharpen our saws. So, Katie and I tried to schedule dates and times away. Thankfully, our parents were willing and eager to help (usually).

At first, we worried about leaving Aedan. When Katie and I had our first date night away from Aedan, we left him with Grandmom, who had successfully raised Katie and her younger sister. Nevertheless, we called four times to see if Aedan was okay. It got easier as time went on, of course. Now we rarely call to check on the kids when they are with their grandparents. Sometimes, when they want to keep the kids for a while longer, we readily agree. So, we no longer feel guilty about taking a night off, or even three days every year, generally around our anniversary.

That said, at the moment of our departure, our babies and toddlers often protested. Their nerves could be calmed by giving them a hug, telling them we loved them, and reminding them that we would return to see them in the morning. Because they had attention spans like a meth dealer who was high on his own supply, we could distract our kids with a colorful toy as we departed. They usually forgot about us.

"Sharpening the Saw" should also involve self-improvement. We have sought ways to become better parents. This might mean reading a book, doing research, or talking with mentors. When Brennan was a toddler, he went through a health crisis (febrile seizures). The first time this happened, Katie and I panicked. We were confused and frightened. As the doctors did their part, I also read everything I could about febrile seizures to make sure I understood what Brennan was going through. The second time he had a seizure, Katie and I panicked a lot less. Katie still called for an ambulance because a Safety-First family believes it is better to be safe than sorry, but she wasn't overtaken by fear.

We talked to many of our friends with children. Sometimes we got bad advice, advice that wouldn't work for our kids, but we always gained a nugget or two of wisdom. Sometimes just venting with a friend was great therapy. Katie and her girlfriends held regular Red Wine Therapy sessions, which they often regretted the next day. My role was to keep the kids away from the ladies, because them bitches were cray-cray by the end of the night.

I found it was better to vent about children with my friends than with my parents. In my experience, parents didn't show a lot of sympathy during venting sessions. I had already made my parents' life a hell, so they thought my parenting struggles were bad karma. Also, our parents loved their grandchildren more than they loved us, which made it harder for them to believe the kids could do anything wrong. I don't blame them. For all these reasons, my parents, at least, did not want to listen to my complaints. "Have a quarter and call someone who cares," they would say, using an ancient phrase with origins in the Payphone Age.

Partnership

I'm fortunate to have a committed partner in my parenting venture. So, when Katie needs a break, I'm partially responsible for making sure she gets one. In practice, this means that I assume responsibility for the boys during Red Wine Therapy, or I arrange for a babysitter. I take an active role in her mental health. If I can't get away with Katie, I encourage her to visit friends for a few days while leaving the kids and house with me. I can usually juggle work, kids, and Tucker for a few days without dropping any balls (probably). It's important for Katie (as the primary caregiver) to get breaks. If she hits the wall, the whole family is screwed.

We also need to maintain our marriage. Our relationship is a catalyst for building our family. When the kids leave home, hopefully our marriage will still be strong. I've been saddened to see my parents' friends get divorces after their kids left home for college or work. Those people seemed to hold their marriages together only for the sake of the kids, not because of each other. Katie and I realized that for our marriage to last, we must put work into it even when the kids are little.

I'm not big on handing out advice, but I like to whip out this advice at weddings: It takes two people to make marriage work, and it takes one person to end it. If both people in the marriage keep trying, the relationship will work. Relationships are about trying and trying until one person dies. As morbid as the thought is, it's true. If one person gives up, the relationship will end. Time to cut bait and move on.

To be clear, I'm not discouraging anyone from ending a relationship and I'm not judging. Every situation is different. I am just trying to bring clarity. It's impossible to build a good relationship and not try. Everyone must try or accept that the relationship is over.

I never want my marriage to end in divorce. That would seem like an awful waste of time—to build something with Katie only to have it all end when our kids leave home. We got married for each other, not just to have kids. If Katie had just wanted kids, she could have chased down a wealthier, more handsome sperm donor than me. Marriages, like plants and children, need nourishment to grow.

When our kids are gone, Katie and I will be stuck with each other (preferably). I'm hoping that life in our fifties will look a lot like life in our twenties: nachos and beer at the bar on Sunday mornings while watching the East Coast football games and wrapping up at 4 p.m. when the afternoon games are over. I'll catch the Sunday night game at home, because I will be in my fifties and therefore unable to drink for the next twelve hours like I could in my twenties.

I want to travel with Katie to golf courses and bass lakes around the US, to enjoy our freedom. I want to reminisce about our kids' hijinks and talk about the great things they will do after college. When they are studying or working, I want them to know that Katie and I had just golfed eighteen holes. I want to talk them into coming home at Thanksgiving—because we miss them. Then Katie and I can watch the sun go down, beers in hand, and know that we survived.

Am I a Good Parent?

Katie and I often wonder if we're good parents. It's probably a good thing to be skeptical about ourselves. Questioning our parenting abilities, behaviors, and methods indicates that we want to improve. But we almost never get positive feedback from others about our parenting. So far, I can only remember one compliment, and that was from the stranger on the flight (see chapter on travel).

Given that I do some things right and a lot of things not-so-right, I've wondered if the rights offset the wrongs. If so, how many rights does it take to offset the wrongs? Will one good bit of parenting compensate for the 1,233,154 times I've screwed up?

Katie and I know plenty of people who have been willing to point out our parenting flaws. She used to join parenting websites, and if she posted a comment or question, she had to prepare to be eviscerated as a horrible parent. Grandparents questioned us constantly, which perhaps implied that we were making bad choices.

Unsolicited advice about how to take care of our children would compel us to tell the advice-giver to "go to the beach and pound all the sand." He or she hadn't been with us night after night, day after day while changing diapers, preparing bottles, reading bedtime stories, and having our souls slowly sucked out of us by an adorable little parasite. The advice-giver had no right to question our methods. In fact, he or she was probably a suck-ass parent who shouldn't be handing out advice at all.

But Katie and I still hear that nagging little voice ask, *Am I a good parent?*

Once upon a time, most parenting advice came from grandparents, relatives, and neighbors who managed to live long enough to impart wisdom. The average lifespan in places like ancient Greece or Rome was around twenty-eight years, so if parents in that era could find someone who made it into their forties or fifties, they probably gained some sound advice, such as, "Don't wander around the woods at night," or "Have ten babies because half of them will die," or "Don't pull on Superman's cape, because that guy has a wicked right cross." Perhaps those people were lucky enough to not get hit with a stray arrow or catch one of that era's many nasty plagues.

In modern times, parents have plentiful resources from experts. Knowing how to parent should, therefore, be an open-and-shut case, a simple matter of checking off the boxes. Even though I should be #winning, I still have my doubts.

The upside is that those doubts help me think beyond the child's physical needs. Having a "healthy" baby is the bare minimum of what I want for my kids. At a deeper level, I want to raise happy, well-adjusted human beings who will contribute to society and not become mass-murdering psychopaths. I also want our kids to grow up and give us grandchildren.

#winning

So, the question "Am I a good parent?" is primarily about the intellectual and emotional development of my children. How do I judge that? If I were to score myself, which measures should I use?

On a scale of one to ten, I'm intellectually a six. I know this because I work and vote like a real adult. Emotionally, I'm a three. I know this because I play video games while wearing my adult-size He-Man pajamas, and because I cried during my last *Call of Duty* game because of #cheating.

Reference points for parenting self-assessment are hard to find. I have tried to come up with objective definitions for what it means to be a good parent, but my criteria has conflicted with the definitions of other people. Some parents spank their children to help them understand the consequences of breaking rules thereby helping the child, in the future, avoid jail time for robbing a liquor store. Other parents never correct their children and only intervene when a kid is doing something that could cause physical harm, such as setting fire to a house. These parents prefer to teach their kids by being good examples. Who's right? Well, an internet search about spanking, for example, will generate thousands of conflicting articles. My point is that two completely reasonable adults will approach parenting with opposite tactics while pursuing the same goal: to raise a responsible, respectable adult.

For this reason, I find it hard to score parenting skills. What measure should I use? How do I objectively judge my efforts when there are no clear measures for how to do the job.

Lacking reference points, some parents measure their abilities by waiting to see how their kids turn out. This approach is also not foolproof. Is a lawyer better than a car mechanic? What if the lawyer beats his wife, but the mechanic works at the soup kitchen every other Thursday? What if the lawyer beats his wife, but donates 10 percent of his sizable income to combat child trafficking? Do the lawyer's good deeds cancel out his bad behaviors? What if the mechanic likes to jerk off to midget porn?

Then there is the nature versus nurture debate. Simply put, how much of a child's behavior, intelligence, and responsible-adult behavior is tied to inherited genetics (nature) versus the lessons she or he learned during childhood (nurture)? Will my role as a parent matter and, if so, how much will it count?

To tease out the influence of nature versus nurture, researchers have studied adopted children to learn how much their behaviors reflect the birth parents' characteristics (nature) versus their adoptive parents' influence (nurture). Researchers have also studied twins (identical and fraternal) to discover how genetics might affect behavior. (Identical twins have a 100 percent genetic match, but fraternal twins have a 50 percent genetic match.)

The general consensus among researchers is that about half of a child's behavior is genetic and about half is learned. Researchers emphasize that nurture factors interact with nature factors; they are interrelated. In other words, the answer to the question of whether a child's struggles in school are genetic or environmental is yes. Science doesn't provide much clarity for day-to-day parenting decisions.

As a father, therefore, I'm on the hook, sort of, for how my children turn out. My nurturing efforts are immensely important, but so are factors like genetics. Perhaps it's best to recognize that each child comprises the genes and the nurturing they have received. My job as a father is to do the best I can with the nurturing.

I Can't Control Everything

I know one thing: To be a good parent, I must show up. I must be present. If half of my kids' behavior is influenced by their environment, then I need to create that environment. I need to understand each child well enough to raise him according to his individual traits.

That said, when I show up, I bring my own traits to the game. I'm an individual with nature and nurture influences. I react to situations and circumstances in unique ways. It's important for me to be aware of myself and how I relate to other people. So, I take stock of myself and my behavior because I don't want to be an asshole.

Being self-aware doesn't mean that I only think about all the ways I suck. I know I have terrible flaws. For example, I worry a lot. I expend a lot of energy hashing and rehashing worst-case scenarios. I talk constantly talk about gloom and doom, which bores Katie to death and keeps me up at night. Why should I spend time and energy obsessing about things outside my control? Worrying is only helpful if I can take action to solve the problem. Worrying wastes my time if the solutions and outcomes are beyond my control. Therefore, I must remind myself of the things I do well and the things I can control. For example, I can show up. I can show up for work and offer my maximum effort every day. I can come home after work every night to help make dinner and parent the kids.

I could make other choices. I could hit a bar

every night to build relationships with customers, vendors, and coworkers. Sometimes that stuff is part of my job. But doing that every day would prevent me from being a present father and husband. I want to be home. I should be home. I don't want to wake up in ten years and realize I missed my kids' childhood.

Since I'm going to be there, I try to bring something good to the table, *something I can control,* such as having a good attitude. I confess that I often fail. When the kids are going nuts, throwing poopy diapers off the balcony, coloring on the walls, and telling Katie "I'd rather die than eat this chicken," it's hard to maintain a positive attitude. I'm even tempted to blame them for my grumpy demeanor. I also don't like assigning pushups, taking away privileges, and lecturing them about bad behavior. I'd rather play video games, drink beer, go fishing, or even mow the lawn. However, as a parent, it is part of my duty to correct them. It's part of showing up. Leaving it all to Katie would be unfair. It would be unfair to the kids (and everyone else) if we never instructed or corrected our children. Someone must teach them, and it should be Katie and me, not SpongeBob.

That's why I show up.

Epilogue

One terrifying final thought: Raising babies and toddlers is simultaneously a long and short trip. On the one hand, having a baby and being on the hook for that person is a huge commitment. On the other hand, eighteen years fly by fast.

Soon I'll be asking, *What the heck happened?* This realization inspires me to hug my sons, and to hug them *now,* and to spend time with them. When they were younger, I would break out the Legos and build something with them. When they are older, I'll bug them about giving me grandchildren. And when I have grandchildren, I'll hug them too.

Time is the most valuable thing we have, and time is best spent with family and friends. Katie and I recently celebrated our tenth wedding anniversary. We watched the video of our wedding, which was one of the best days of our lives. But watching the video was bittersweet. We saw many family members who were at that wedding, like Katie's dad, who are no longer with us. It was a snapshot in time that can never be repeated.

Our time with our babies and toddlers can't be repeated either. It can only be survived.

CPSIA information can be obtained
at www.ICGtesting.com
Printed in the USA
FSHW011812121220
76671FS